NMZ
BOOKS

Copyright © 2021 by NO MANS ZONE
Publishing history: Edition 2017, 2018, 2019, 2020
Cover Design by NO MANS ZONE

All Scripture quotations in this publication are from the New Revised Standard Version. Copyright 1989, Division of Christian Education of the National Council of the Churches of Christ in the United States unless otherwise indicated.

Publisher's Disclaimer

All rights reserved. No portion of this publication may be reproduced, stored in an electronic system, or transmitted in any form or by any means, electronic, mechanical, photocopy, recording, or otherwise, without permission in writing from the publisher. Brief quotations may be used in literary reviews. Whilst every care has been taken to ensure the accuracy of the material contained herein, neither the author nor the publisher or its agents will accept responsibility or liability for any action taken by any person, persons, or organization claimed to be in whole or in part upon the information contained herein.

Proceeds from the publication, distribution, and sale of this book are received as gifts to NO MANS ZONE.

ISBN 9798447305871

Published by
NO MANS ZONE
PO BOX 3444
Apia
Samoa 685
www.nomanszone.org

A publication of

NOMANSZONE

MEMORY

In memory of my Father
Richard Vincent Meredith.

A great visionary of his time.

DEDICATION

This Book is dedicated to my son Joseph Meredith. May it cause you to realize the Destiny that GOD has given you, my son, and the destiny of your sons and their sons.

It is also dedicated to YOU, my friend, so that you can realize your destiny!

THANK YOU

A very special thank you to my wife, Marjorie Grace Meredith, for the work she has put into critiquing, reviewing, and checking this book and for taking care of our family and our ministry so that I can dedicate my time to GOD's service. This book is as much the fruit of her labors as it is mine.

CONTENTS

Preface	1
Introduction	3
Chapters	
1 The Power of vision	7
2 The Character of vision	13
3 The Logistics of vision	24
4 The Properties of vision	34
5 The Nature of vision	46
6 The Process of vision	57
7 The Pitfalls of vision	65
8 The Vices of vision	78
9 The Incubation of vision	87
Summary	108
About the Author	110
NMZ Releases	111
Notes	112

It is somewhat ironic that we understand more today about the products of vision but not vision itself.

PREFACE

Is there a power on Earth that is more powerful than the torrents of the Niagara Falls or the shifting currents of the Pacific Ocean? What about the force of a 240 mile an hour hurricane or the strength of an 8 Richter scale earthquake. Can we hardly compare? Yet, there is a power that is more powerful than any physical or natural phenomena. So powerful that it is responsible for creating devices that can now literally obliterate mankind. What can this power be? It is VPower, *the power of vision.* Yes, vision created the atomic bomb, the nuclear bomb, and the neutron bomb. Before these inventors or discoverers created these devices, a vision created the pathway to accomplish it. Yet vision is also equally responsible for making all the technologies and advancements that preserve and promote life today.

It is somewhat ironic that we understand more today about the products of vision but not vision itself. Perhaps this ignorance stems from the fact that there are relatively few books dedicated to the topic. It is my vision that when you read this book, you will not only understand the mechanics of vision but that you will become a person of vision. I believe that this book is a key that I am placing into your hands that will unlock that immense and limitless potential that you were born with that only GOD/UNIVERSE gave you. There is a mover of mountains in every man waiting to be released by this key I have titled VPower. Read this book with an expectation to receive! And expect to be moved to go to places or heights you thought were not possible!

A short note to my many friends from around the World who will read this book. As you read through this book, many of the examples I use are from my own background and region of the World where I was born, the Pacific Islands, so I ask you to excuse my bias but not excuse the lessons.

A word on the name "GOD" I will be using in this book.

I have used the substitute "GOD" in capital letters as a substitute for the Tetragram.

In Hebrew, the Set-Apart name comprises four letters יהוה pronounced as Yud י, Hei ה, Vav ו, Hei ה. This is referred to as the "Tetragram" or Tetragrammaton," meaning roughly "The Four letters."

For my friends who are atheists or agnostics, you may prefer to say the Universe, so that option is noted throughout alongside the word GOD – GOD/UNIVERSE where it is appropriate.

Vision gives us the ability to see farther and before others do in our time.

INTRODUCTION

I have always wondered how a man with no more than a high school level of education can hardly speak a word in English, and with only a few thousand dollars, can come into a western democracy, start a business and become a millionaire after five or so years. Further, it still baffles me how a man who has a University level of education, speaks perfect English, and has thousands of dollars at his disposal to operate a business in the same democratic system but cannot make it in business. My father was a businessman who had no more than a secondary or high school level of education, but by the time he was in his forties, he had made his first million and was one of the few millionaires in my country. This was during the 1970s. I was raised up living on top of eight different factories that my father had built. All of which he had started from scratch and built up to be leading businesses in my country. Among the businesses that my father began was a store, a bread factory, a biscuit factory, a lolly factory, a printing press, a paint factory, a meat factory, and a coconut cream factory. There were other businesses that my father went into partnership with others, but his dying aspiration was to start a bank, which eventuated after his death.

My father had no special training in any of the businesses he started, nor did he have any formal education in business, but he had a way of acquiring friends who would help him start these ventures. Many would put my father's success to luck or chance, others to his business accruement or foresight, and still others to his business acquaintances or contacts. However, I have come to discover that the real secret of my father's success did not lie in any of these factors, although it had assisted him; but *it was in his ability to see farther and before others could see in his time. We call this VISION.* My father was a man of vision, which enabled him to be a step ahead of many of his time's business companions. Most of my father's operations were not original in concept or idea but were unique in my country. Over the years, I have witnessed many business graduates from foreign Universities; return home to my country only to spend the rest of their years working for Government departments or business people who, like my father, had no University level of education. Not that there is anything wrong with this.

> *Vision gives us the ability to see farther and before others do in our time.*

My wife and I recently had a wonderful opportunity to travel to the Islands of the South Seas to do a documentary for a Christian Television Network of which we are part. Our travels took us to the Solomon Islands, Vanuatu, Fiji, Tonga, Samoa, and the Cook

Islands. In each of these countries, we noticed a distinct group of individuals who had come into these Island nations from foreign nations and set up a business and were now monopolizing many of the trade and industry in these Islands. In some countries like Fiji and the Solomon Islands, 90 percent of the business activities were dominated by immigrants instead of native Islanders. Being a native Islander of Samoan and English descent and a local businessman, I was intrigued by how this had happened and why fewer native citizens of these countries were in business. I knew the difficulties of a foreigner coming in and establishing a business was far more significant than a native citizen of that country. For one thing, a foreigner had a language barrier and a cultural barrier to overcome than a native citizen did not have. Furthermore, foreigners had more Government red tape to overcome than the local people had to face.

Like my father, many of these business immigrants had only a secondary or high school level of education. If they had a degree, it was in an area with no relevance in business. For instance, one man I met who had become a multi-millionaire had initially entered my country as a medical doctor but was now a very successful retailer. Some of these immigrants still could not speak English and found it more comfortable conversing in the native language. I could not imagine what could have brought these people to the Islands, but it was apparent that they succeeded in an area where the native people were not. What was it that caused these people to succeed and had sustained them in obviously a challenging environment? The answer is vision.

Some of us may contend that it was because these foreigners had the money or the influence or the experience that was the driving force that made them successful. The truth is money, influence, and experience can only take a person so far, but the rest of the way, it has to be something far more powerful and enduring than what we bring with us that fortifies a person never to give in or give up. A blind woman was asked a very portent question, "What could be worse than being blind?" She answered, "Having sight but no vision."

The driving force behind any successful person in the past or the present, or the future, has been and is and will be vision.

CHAPTER ONE

The Power of Vision

I have a plague in my father's house that states, "A fool and his money are soon parted." Money in the hands of a man who has a vision is a powerful combination, but money in the hands of a man who has no vision is a foolish combination. Even worse still is money in the hands of a man who is an educated fool. An education is a good thing to have, but it is certainly not a guarantee that you will succeed. In fact, most of the problems we have in the World today were created by educated people. The more educated we have become, the more difficult it has become to solve the many political, social, and economic problems we have in the World today. Therefore, the answer does not lie in how many letters we place behind our names on a business card but in understanding the revolutionary power of vision. Show me any successful man in the World today who is leading in any field of endeavor, and I will prove to you that man has a vision. Show me any successful woman in the World today who is leading in any field of endeavor, and I will prove to you that woman has a vision. *The driving force behind any successful person in the past or the present, or the future, has been and is and will be vision.*

> *The driving force behind any successful person in the past or the present, or the future, has been and will be vision.*

We have many gifted and talented artists in our little region of the World. Most of them will never get international recognition for their gift and talent. However, it never ceases to amaze me how a man from a primitive bush background with only a rudimentary level of education can carve a wood or stone statute with such precision detail that makes Leonardo Davinci's statutes look like elementary artwork. Just recently, the Maori people of New Zealand were displaying their native artwork in New York, and many marveled at how such a so-called primitive Pacific culture can come up with such intricate and detailed artwork. This is the power of vision. When people are driven by vision, what is to one man, a lifeless stone, or a simple old tree is material for an incredible masterpiece. When a carver who has a vision stands before a tree, in his mind, he sees the statue in the tree as though the tree were made for the statue. In the confines of the carver's mind, the dimensions and curvatures of the statue are not a factor to be discovered or worked out. He already knows what it is, as though the vision had downloaded this information into his mind.

The power of vision enables a man to change and shape his environment. You can give a pig farmer ten thousand dollars and come back a year later, and his farm is no better than what it was the year before. But give that same farmer the ten thousand dollars with a vision, and next year you will see a ham factory. We live in a community, in a society, in a culture, and in a country that was shaped by vision. Whether directly or indirectly, vision has affected and transformed our lives. We will never meet the man who invented the automobile, or the man who invented the airplane, or the man who invented the train because they are all in the grave, but every day our lives are being transformed and improved by their visions. Also, we take for granted the many little conveniences we enjoy that make our lives so much better, for example, a toaster, a coffee machine, a juice blender, a blow dryer, an electric fan, etc. Most of which we cannot do without today. These wonderful little conveniences are all products of vision. In fact, it would not be an exaggeration to state that everything that our five senses can evidence, what we see, hear, taste, feel and smell, is a product of a vision. Everyday vision is touching and shaping our lives, whether you are aware of it or not, or whether you approve of it or not. There is no escape in this World from the touch of vision.

Have you ever watched an Eagle fly? They are magnificent creatures to watch. They can glide effortlessly on a desert wind for hours and have you mesmerized. We do not have eagles in our part of the World, but we have a few comparable-sized sea birds that can glide just as effortlessly for hours over miles of deep Blue Ocean. While fishing, I have sometimes sat for hours and watched these masters of flight glide and slide in the wind. Even though I cannot see the force that drives the bird up and down, I know that the bird is not up there because of an event of chance. The invisible force that lifts the bird into the air is the power of the wind. So it is the same with the soul of a man who has a vision. *The invisible force that lifts a man into souring heights in life is the power of vision. The most powerful thing that a man can have is a vision.* If you want your personal life transformed, get a vision. If you're going to transform a community or a society, or a nation, give people a vision. The most dangerous thing you can personally do to yourself is to become a visionary. What our World desperately needs today are more visionaries.

I often make a habit of looking at cemeteries when I drive by. The reason being is because I believe that cemeteries are the wealthiest places on Earth. It's not because of the gold or diamonds that the dead take with them into their graves or the treasures they have hidden in safety deposit boxes or bank accounts they forgot to tell their living relatives, but it is because of the millions of "unrealized visions" that people take with them to their grave. How many of us have had the privilege of being with a loved one on their final days. At this time, the dying often gives an insight into what they had aspired to do or achieve but were not able to because time had run out of time? My father passed away when I was in my thirties, and to my

> *The invisible force that lifts a man into souring heights in life is the power of vision. The most powerful thing that a man can have is a vision.*

disappointment, I was not around when he passed. I often think of what my father could have achieved in his life if he only lived another twenty years. One of his dying aspirations was to start a bank, and he died before this vision was realized. A man once made a very powerful statement that has never left me. He said, "when I die, I want to die empty." What he meant was that he wanted to accomplish every vision that he had received before he died. What a way to go!

Many years ago, I met a man and his wife, who has a vision that they would build for GOD a Christian Television Network that would cover the globe. At that time, I was part of their operations to broadcast into the South Pacific, and as a result, they came to visit my tiny Island. Their names were Paul and Jan Crouch, the founder of Trinity Broadcasting Network (TBN), who has since passed away. Here is a little background on their vision. TBN is the world's largest Christian television network and America's most-watched faith-and-family channel. TBN today is a growing family of over thirty global networks reaching every inhabited continent with a broad range of inspirational, entertaining, and life-changing programming twenty-four hours a day. In the U.S., TBN's family of networks is available to 98 percent of television households, and globally TBN reaches an estimated two billion potential viewers each day! Matt Crouch their son currently serves as TBN's president and head of operations.

When I met Paul Crouch his operation was not as far reaching as it is today, I could see that a powerful vision drove this man and his wife. I understood he would not go to the grave until he had achieved his dream, and he did it and surpassed it to the glory of GOD. It was through Paul Crouch that I got involved in television and radio broadcasting for many years. I am forever thankful for the many gifts they gave to me.

Some concluding thoughts

I don't know why people make things so complicated these days; I guess people need to have jobs so that they can sell this, buy that, borrow this or lend that to get busy. The truth is all we need to get is vision, and believe it or not! It does not cost you anything to get a vision. The fact is without vision, people don't go anywhere, and people who are heading somewhere are driven by vision. Most Governments believe that we need more education, while most Law Makers believe that we need more laws and most Religions believe that we need more religion, while most Industries believe that we need more stuff, yet when we look at the World today, there are more economic problems, more wars, more crime, and more unhappy people today even though education, law, religion, and commodities have increased by 1000 percent since the middle ages. What we don't need is more products but for people to have vision and not any vision but visions that have character because not all vision will have character.

The heart of the vision is the DREAM that inspired and created the vision.

CHAPTER TWO

The Character of Vision

All sorts of people go fishing these days, but there are really only two types of fishermen. One who knows what he is doing and one who thinks he knows what he is doing. What distinguishes "the know" from "the think" is not the type of tackle box or brand of fishing rod they are using but the character and the nature of their vision. Two fishermen arrive at the dock with a vision to catch fish, at least most fishermen do, but one walks away with a bucket full of fish and the other with a fish story. Why did one fisherman succeed and the other fail? The difference between success and failure lies in the character of their vision. The character can be briefly defined as the spine or backbone of something. The vision characters are those underlying internal qualities that make up the spine or backbone of the vision. A vision that has character will always have these three immutable and universal qualities. The vision will have:

1 A HEART.

2 A PURPOSE.

3 & A DESTINY.

The *Heart* of the vision

The heart of the vision is the DREAM that inspired and created the vision. Every vision has a dreamer who has a dream that inspires the visionary. The dream is the source that creates the visionary, but it is the visionary who has the vision to fulfill the dream. Hence the heart of vision is the dream.

Dreamer ⇨ Dream ⇨ Visionary ⇨ Vision

> The heart of the vision is the DREAM that inspired and created the vision.

In the early nineteenth century, around the 1800s, a host of European settlers migrated to the Pacific Islands. What on Earth motivated these people to come to these islands with little or nothing to offer them except an inexhaustible supply of coconuts and sand? This had always intrigued me? One of these settlers was my great, great, great grandfather, who came from Wales, England. He boarded a schooner somewhere in Wales and went to the Islands with a dream to make it as a trader. I do not doubt that it was his parents who had first put this dream into his heart because of the so many success stories that were circulating in England from her newly founded colonies of America, Australia, and New Zealand. The news had leaked out that the newest frontier were the Islands, and they were ready for the picking. No one in his right mind would just board a boat and come to the Pacific unless they were inspired by something greater than themselves; a dream.

It was not long before my great, great, great grandfather found himself a native wife, my great, great, great grandmother, and started a store and a small bakery. Their dream impacted and inspired my father to start a bakery and a biscuit factory. Other settlers who had come during the same time as my great, great, great grandfather also started businesses and are now the leading business families in my country. These founding fathers from England or Europe or Asia came to the Pacific with a dream that is the catalyst of today's visionaries. Martin Luther King coined and popularised that immortal phrase, "I have a dream," and what a dream this man had. America had decreed in its Constitution that all men were created free and equal. When Martin Luther King made, this statement blacks and whites were still legally segregated as late as the 1960s, yet emancipation of slavery occurred in America in 1865. That dream birthed a tremendous political movement in America and birthed thousands of black and white activists who have championed the cause of freedom in America to this day. The dream was what created and inspired the visionaries, and it was the visionaries who moved the mountains.

It is essential that we see this distinction between a dreamer and a visionary before going further. *A dreamer is the source or the nest from which the visionaries are birthed. The dreamers are the mothers and fathers of visionaries.* The visionary, the child, is the resource that fulfills the dream. Dreamers rarely ever get fully acknowledged for their contribution because their contribution is often intangible and in the background. They are the ones who persist with you when everyone else said, "you cannot do it, or it is not possible"; they are the ones who break down the so-called walls of myths and legends that previous people had created to justify their failures. Any person who has had a positive and life-changing influence on you was the dreamer that inspired you to be the visionary you are today. Some of today's greatest visionaries were born on the lap of a grandfather or a grandmother or in the classroom of a teacher or a coach who never gave up on them despite what everybody else said about them. There is always that special person or persons whose actions are directly responsible for the visionaries of yesterday and today.

> *A dreamer is the source or the nest from which the visionaries are birthed. The dreamers are the mothers and fathers of visionaries.*

Why dreamers never turn into visionaries is not really important because we will always need our dreamers. The visionaries' mistake in life is not to acknowledge or reward the dreamer for their dream. For some of us, it may not be possible to do this because this particular dreamer or dreamers may no longer be around, but it should never stop us from acknowledging their contribution in some way. For instance, a Memorabilia dedicated in their honor to the building they inspired you to build. A letter of acknowledgment framed in the foyer of your office, buying a brick in their honor at the dedication of a building, publishing an article in the newspapers acknowledging their contribution, dedicating a book in their honor, etc. There are literally hundreds of creative ways one can recognize the contribution of these dreamers. On the other hand, no real dreamer will tell a visionary that they want to be acknowledged because this was never the reason. If a dreamer ever seeks acknowledgment from a visionary for their contribution, they are likely to have never really influenced the visionary. The dreamers that inspired my father were, no doubt, my grandfather and grandmother.

The *Purpose* of the vision

Purpose can be defined as the intended end or result of an action. *A vision must have an intended end or result. A vision without a purpose is a vision that has no character.* Anything that has no character, i.e. spine or backbone, will not last the distance. It is crucial that we know and understand the purpose of the vision. This should be clear at the outset of the vision and not something that we are struggling to identify later in the vision. During the time when my father was contemplating starting a bakery and biscuit factory, many other business people in my country had a similar vision, but only two men succeeded at that time. At that time, the monetary and economic conditions were basically the same for everyone in my country. If you had some freehold land, you could borrow some money and start a business. My father's success had nothing to do with his time's prevailing economic or monetary factors, but it had to do with the fact that he had a clear purpose to his vision. My father may not have had the most admirable and honorable purpose, but because he had a purpose, and it made all the difference to his vision.

My father's purpose was threefold. First, he wanted to be a millionaire; second, he wanted to provide a better future for his family; and third, he wanted to do better than his father had done and proved him wrong. We all have our reasons, but these reasons are the very purpose why the vision eventuates, and it is perpetuated to succeeding generations but not necessarily why it succeeds or fails. Some people have a wrong purpose to their vision, yet they succeed, and some people have a good purpose to their visions, yet they fail. Purpose of itself does not guarantee that a vision will succeed, but what it does is put a perspective or a goal into the vision that will ensure its long-term survival. Without a purpose in your vision, the vision will become meaningless. When something is meaningless, it will not have an aim or a goal or a reason for its existence. Every activity that occurs in the realm of nature has a purpose to it. Things do not happen because of chance despite some evolutionary claims. There is a purpose why a leaf loses its glory and falls gracefully to the ground. There is a purpose why rocks break down into pebbles then decay into meaningless sand. We may not understand its mechanics, but we know that it is necessary for life to continue to exist. So is a purpose to the life of the vision.

> A vision must have an intended end or result. A vision without a purpose is a vision that has no character.

> *A vision that has an outward-looking purpose envisages the good of others over the good of its founders. An inward-looking vision will always seek the primary good of itself or its founders over betterment of others.*

When the vision has character, it will have *an outward-looking purpose,* and when a vision does not have character, it will have *an inward-looking purpose.* A vision that has an outward-looking purpose envisages the good of others over the good of its founders. An inward-looking vision will always seek the primary good of itself or its founders over others' betterment. A vision with an outward purpose improves, changes for the good or impacts for the good, the state or condition or wellbeing of others. Consider, for example, two men who both have a simple vision to buy a car. The purpose of one man in buying his car is for his job and his family. The other man's purpose for buying a car is for show and himself. The purpose of their vision determines the destiny of their vision. The man who buys his car for his job and family has the greater good of others in mind, while the man who buys his car for himself only has his good in mind. Thus, the first man has an outward-looking vision, and the second man has an inward-looking vision. The outward-looking vision impacts and improves the condition of others, while the inward-looking vision benefits only itself. Which of these visions had a destiny?

Now it is entirely possible to have a vision without a purpose. Take, for example, a young man who happens to be a nephew of mine who is a very bright and capable young man. Six years ago, he embarked on a University education. A quarter way through his degree, he changes his mind and starts another degree; halfway through this degree, he switches to another degree. I am sure you have this sort in your own family. After sitting down with my nephew and looking back at his track record, it does not take a genius to figure out that this young man had no purpose. He had a vision to receive a University degree, but what kind of degree was something he never sorted out. What was the result of this? A purposeless or meaningless vision. What was the cost of this? Wasted opportunity and money. Unfortunately, this is a common problem among University entrants today, and there is a cost to these meaningless visions. During my University years, nearly all of my classmates I had gone to secondary or high school graduated with-in the standard three years. We all had a purpose for our vision. The thinking of this generation may have changed, but the result is never different. A vision must have a purpose.

The *Destiny* of the vision

The destiny of the vision is its moral and humane impact. The general good or improvement that it will do to future generations. A visionary will have many visions, but not all of those visions will have a destiny. Only a vision that has a destiny will have character. The word destiny means "appointed or preordained." It means that there is a greater power behind the vision other than our human design. I call this "the GOD/UNIVERSE factor of vision." When you have the GOD/UNIVERSE factor in your vision, you know, without a doubt, that your vision has a destiny, a divine destiny. When you realize this, you know you cannot fail because you are destined to succeed. The GOD/UNIVERSE factor is the inspiration behind the vision. Two of the greatest inventors of the Ninetieth Century, Benjamin Franklin and Thomas Edison, were devout Christians. Benjamin Franklin invented the bifocal (glasses), lightning rod, iron furnace stove, and odometer. Thomas Edison patented 1,093 inventions, the most famous of his inventions being the light bulb. Edison was quoted as saying, "Genius is one percent inspiration and 99 percent perspiration." It is this one percent, the GOD/UNIVERSE factor, that was responsible for the destiny of these men and their inventions. There are very few people on this Earth who are not affected by the destiny of these men's inventions.

> *The destiny of the vision is its moral and humane impact. The general good or improvement that it will do to future generations.*

The GOD/UNIVERSE factor does three things to the vision. First, it puts an *eternal perspective* into the vision. You know that there is a greater power at work in your vision other than your human design and ingenuity. Second, it provides *hope* to vision. You know something greater than yourself urges you to pursue and persevere when everybody else has given up. Third, the GOD/UNIVERSE factor puts *humility* into the vision. You know that without GOD/UNIVERSE, you could not have done it. *The GOD/UNIVERSE factor in vision is about a partnership between*

GOD/UNIVERSE and man. A professional rope maker will confirm that the strongest rope is made out of a Threefold strand because only under this combination do all the three strands attach themselves to each other. When GOD/UNIVERSE and man and vision are attached together, it is an unbreakable and unshakable combination. Literally, all things are possible. D L Moody, a famous evangelist of the 19th Century, is reported to have said to his sons on his deathbed. "If God be your partner, make your plans large." I have a plague on my desk that states, "If you can do it, GOD's not in it." Well, at this point, some of you may be asking, what if I am an atheist. Perhaps it is time to reconsider your position. Can you honestly say that there is no GOD? To arrive at this position, a person must state that they have searched every corner of this World and did not find GOD. What atheists can honestly say that they have done this? Never the less I understand your angle. Perhaps it would be better for you to look at the GOD/UNIVERSE factor as the Universe factor because you cannot remove the unseen forces behind the vision that drives it. It is always there, like gravity that pulls and pushes matter.

> *The GOD/UNIVERSE factor in vision is about a partnership between GOD/UNIVERSE and man.*

Some concluding thoughts

A visionary will have many visions, but only a few of these visions will ever make it into the hallways of destiny. People rarely ever remember the great business exploits or accomplishments of men of previous generations. For example, if I were to ask you to name a couple of the greatest businessmen of the Ninetieth Century in your own country, we would sincerely struggle with such an exercise unless you happen to be a historian. However, if I asked you who founded a hospital, a school, a university, a library, or a theme park, you would probably know in your country. Why? Because their vision had a destiny, and often the achievement is named after their honor. There was a great businessman in my country and was one of those early pioneers or founders who came from Europe to build in the Islands. His name was O F Nelson. By the time he died, he was the richest man in my nation. He started many various businesses and ventures that were instrumental in launching our national economy - for example, the Copra and Coco bean trade and the merchandising industry. Today, most people in my country have no idea of what this man had achieved in his business career. However, most people know him through the public library, which he donated to my people because it bears his name. Others will remember his name in our history books because he was one of the leaders of the famous "Mau" movement that resulted in the independence of my nation from the New Zealand administration. His visions had a destiny because they had a GOD/UNIVERSE factor. That is why we need to put our money, labor, and time into visions that will shape generations. I am quite confident you have such a vision or, if not a dream.

A source is whatever is necessary to start the vision. A vision always starts from a seed; that seed is the source.

CHAPTER THREE

The Logistics of Vision

The logistic of vision is those practical characteristics that make a vision feasible. The word feasible means plausible or possible. The three essential qualities of a feasible vision are:

1 SOURCE.

2 RESOURCE.

3 MANAGEMENT.

Can the vision be sourced?

A source is a place of origination or a point of beginning, for example, a spring or a riverhead. Without the spring, there can be no river. Likewise, every vision has to have a source or sources to start. This source can be money, know-how, labor, materials, or a vehicle, etc. *It is whatever is necessary to start the vision.* When you ask the question of how and where in respect to vision, many people begin to have second thoughts about their vision because they know a vision needs a source or sources to start. Where is the money, know-how, or materials going to come from, what about the labor, etc., they all ask? This may surprise you, but the problem with most of us visionaries is not really the money or know-how or materials. The problem with most of us is that we like to see all of the capital or all of the know-how and all of the materials at the start of the vision, or we allow the finished picture of the vision to overwhelm us or create fear so that we never start. A wise man once said, "Do not despise the day of small beginnings." This is a well-founded statement; everything we see that is big and successful today began from yesterday's little seed. *A vision always starts from a seed; that seed is the source.*

> A source is whatever is necessary to start the vision. A vision always starts from a seed; that seed is the source.

Every vision has a provision. When the vision has a destiny, it will only be a matter of time before the source becomes apparent to the vision. A river will always beat a path to the sea. It is the same with provision for the vision; it will eventually find the visionary. As mentioned during his lifetime, my father started 12 different enterprises, and if he had lived longer, he would have done twice as much. Among the enterprises that my father started were a bakery, a biscuit factory, a lolly factory, a coconut cream processing plant, a meat factory, a paint factory, a printing press, a store, a taxi service, a shipping company, a shoe factory, and a bank. The reason I have re-listed all these enterprises is not so that I can boost in my father's achievements but to show you a key that my father taught me about the source. Every one of these businesses contained different shareholders and produced unrelated products. Yet, they were all sourced in precisely the same manner. My father rarely ever borrowed any capital but got investors to source his vision. As he built up the Company, he re-invested his profits to start the next operation with new shareholders. Some of these shareholders did not come in with money but with the know-how or machinery, or materials he needed to start that business.

> *Every vision has a provision. When the vision has a destiny, it will only be a matter of time before the source becomes apparent to the vision.*

As soon as my father tabled his vision to start a new operation, it did not take him long to find the sources he needed for capital, equipment, and labor. When you live on an Island like my Island, where it takes you no more than half an hour to cross its breadth and two hours to cross its length, you often wonder how some people find the sources they need to start their vision, yet they do it! I am convinced that it has nothing to do with their environment or circumstances, or chance, but it has to do with the fact that provision will always come to the vision. *There will always be a person or persons waiting for the visionary to manifest the vision.* It is almost like a young eagle getting ready to take its first flight. It stands on the edge of its nest, flaps its wings, then plunges forth, and it is instantly caught up by an invincible and powerful force, the wind, and is driven to an amazing height. So is a vision when it is ready to launch forth, it is caught by people who see this vision and want to run with it, so it sores to an amazing height. It is not that these people could not do the vision themselves, but because they know it is not their vision and when the right people do it, it will succeed. Now not all visions have a problem with source; some visions have all the money, technology, and labor it needs but still fail - something we will examine in this next heading.

Can the vision be resourced?

Not so long ago, a couple of businessmen in my country wanted to start a rice mill to counter a growing demand for imported rice and save our country some valuable foreign exchange. They had hoped that the construction of a rice mill would also start a new local industry of growing rice. It was a brilliant business idea and a good development that would help our country. They had the capital and support of the market to start the mill, but they soon disposed of the idea when they discovered that their vision was not feasible. First, the price of imported rice meal compared to finished rice was very marginal; therefore, no short-term profits were foreseeable. Second, our Island's climate was not suited to grow rice; therefore, the possibility of a long-term local rice industry was improbable but not impossible with the right irrigation technology, which will take decades to develop. Even though the vision was sourced because they had the capital and the market's support, the vision was not resourceable. *When the vision is not resourceable, it has no future even though it could be a brilliant or revolutionary idea with all the sources.*

A resource is what is necessary to sustain the vision, what a vision needs to keep it going so that it will not die a natural death after it is sourced.

> *When the vision is not resourceable, it has no future even though it could be a brilliant or revolutionary idea with all its sources.*

Basically, the difference between a source and a resource is as follows. A source is always something that is inputted once to start the vision, but a resource is something that is continually inputted to sustain the vision. Once given, the source creates the resource necessary to maintain the vision, but the source itself does not sustain the vision. We could make many things in our little Island economies that could be cheaper and better because of our inexpensive labor force. However, the number one constraining factor for us is not source but resource. Here in the Islands, some of the most beautiful and succulent fruit on the planet, and many entrepreneurs I have met have the vision to process these fruits into all sorts of exportable commodities that could earn our Islands economies millions of dollars of foreign exchange. Yet it does not happen; why? We do not have the resources of fruit to sustain such a vision. It would take only months to clear every fruit we had on our Island if a fruit processing factory was to open today. In fact, two plants had previously opened and closed down because of this very reason. Also, most of our fruits on the Island are seasonal, so half of the year will be no fruit supply to continue the factory. But what we do have is an abundant and yearly supply of coconuts and nonu, which we currently process and export.

> *A resource is what is necessary to sustain the vision, what a vision needs to keep it going so that it will not die a natural death after it is sourced.*

However, this does not mean that a fruit processing plant cannot be done in the Islands. It is quite possible to operate such a business if one were to plant thousands of hectares of fruit. In fact, some entrepreneurs have done this very thing. For example, in the Solomon Islands, there is a palm oil plant that processes and exports palm oil. Before the plant was built, thousands of hectares of palm trees were planted and are continually being planted for this very purpose. These people knew that for their vision to succeed, they needed to answer this question of resource. *Without a continuous resource or resources to sustain the vision, it will simply die a natural death.* Now and then, we hear of someone raising millions of dollars from some scheme or plan they invented and then hear two years or so later of the collapse of that scheme or plan. They got the sources but soon discovered there were no resources to sustain the thing, so it fell apart. A vision will always stand and fall on the question of resources more than sources. A successful vision will always answer this question of the resource before it starts. When it does not answer this question, it would be best not to start but to tarry until this question is firmly resolved.

Can the vision be managed?

> *Without a continuous resource or resources to sustain the vision it will simply die a natural death.*

I have come across many business ventures throughout my travels in the Pacific, some costing millions of dollars that had closed up after a few years of operation because the venture proved unmanageable. One such project was a coconut fiber mill that they constructed in the Kingdom of Tonga during the 1980s with foreign aid. It was intended that this project would earn Tonga some sizable foreign exchange and create much income for the local people. Today the mill lies completely rusted as a monument to a vision that was not manageable. Many similar projects of this nature were enacted with foreign aid throughout the Islands that are now a testimony to the folly of an unmanageable vision. These projects' intentions may have been good and admirable, but because the vision could not be managed, it created harm and loss in the end. Valuable taxpayer's money and resources were expended in those projects that could have potentially done well elsewhere. As an economist would say, there is an opportunity cost to these projects that can never be recovered. Also, some people were trained and employed by these projects who lost their jobs, and families that depended on these new industries suffered from the loss of their livelihood.

Now when I say that the vision could not be managed, I am not referring to the lack of management or over management. On the contrary, the above projects had qualified managers, but they still failed. What I am referring to is the question of who is capable and able to manage the vision. By management, I mean who can control, coordinate, and administer the vision effectively. *A vision will stand or fall on this issue of management.* Without resolving this question, it will be sheer folly to think of starting. There are many qualified managers in the marketplace, but not all who classify themselves as management can manage. Managing is both a skill and a passion. I have seen companies, ministries, and organizations fall with so-called qualified managers. It happens every day. Unless a manager has the passion, the heart, and the visionary's commitment, the visionary would be better off managing his own vision. Finding such people are as rare as rubies. When a vision is being birthed, it is at its most acute state; therefore, management is at its most critical level. Often it is at this level that all sorts of sacrifices are called to be made, and a visionary needs to ask himself if the people that he is considering are prepared to make these sacrifices if they are called upon. Often, the answer is no.

That is why most Indians and Chinese visionaries who come into places like the Pacific opt to manage their own vision because they cannot find people able to make these sacrifices other than themselves. So inevitably, they succeed. However, later when the vision has taken root, they bring in additional management. When the vision has established itself, they will train a replacement or a descendant to take

> *A vision will stand or fall on the issue of management.*

over. However, not every vision does this because some visions demand a level of expertise and capital investment that the visionary may not have himself. Therefore, the visionary needs to consider whether the applicant can fulfill the requirements of managing this vision. Often this will then boil down to the question of qualification and experience. Is this person qualified and experienced enough to control, coordinate, and administer this vision? These are important technical issues that must be answered. Still, the more important question is whether this person can receive the visionary's passion, heart, and commitment. Can he or she receive or is prepared to obtain from the visionary these qualities that are so essential to the success of the vision? Sometimes this is more difficult to accomplish and can be just as expensive as a provision. Good people are not cheap and easy to find. Usually, the ideal people to take over are those who have worked and sacrificed alongside the visionary.

Some concluding thoughts

Logic really has to do with being practical or down to Earth. Unfortunately, people often get carried away with the flare, glare, and hype of having a vision that we fail to see the reality of implementing the vision. Many years ago, I liked watching wrestling matches on television, and one of the sayings that stuck to my mind that this particular wrestler and his promoters would often say in their pre-match warm-up talk was, "it is time for a rude awaking!" Logistics is about having "a rude awaking" about your vision that comes from answering these preliminary questions of source, resource, and management before you go on any further with the vision. It does not cost any money to get a few facts or information needed to answer these essential questions. A few phone calls to the right people, a visit to the statistics or natural resource department, etc., could well provide you with all the preliminary answers you are looking for. Be warned that if you hit a brick wall, it certainly does not mean that it is all over. It could just mean that the time is not right or that you are in the wrong place to achieve your vision. These will be issues that I will discuss in another section called the vices of vision, but for now, we need to understand some basic fundamentals about the properties of vision because not all we receive qualify as a vision.

*A vision is a medium of exchange
because it is transferable.*

CHAPTER FOUR

The Properties of Vision

The properties of vision are those attributes or qualities that are universal to vision. These are factors that every vision must have, with-out which a vision cannot be classified or categorized as vision. The three essential properties of vision are. A vision must be:

1 TRANSFERABLE   **2** DOCUMENTABLE   **3** ADAPTABLE

Can the vision be transferred?

For something to qualify as a medium of exchange, it must be transferable. We cannot use buildings and land as a medium of exchange because they cannot be physically transferred. Note, I did not say legally transferred but physically transferred. So we use commodities like money, gold, silver, diamonds, etc., as mediums of exchange because they can be transferred easily and simply. *A vision is a medium of exchange because it is transferable.* A vision can be passed on to as many people as are prepared to receive it. However, this does not make the recipient of the vision a visionary but only a carrier of that vision. My wife and I were the pioneers of the first Christian radio station in my country but, we were not the visionary of this radio station. It was a missionary from the United States of America who had the vision to start a radio station in my country who had brought the vision to us. We were the recipients of his vision, but he was not the builder of the vision. His time with us was so brief, being only six months, that there was hardly sufficient time to establish the vision. It was my wife and me who built the vision and firmly established it in my country. Today that radio station has helped build other radio stations and has grown to include television. No one in my nation remembers this man, but they all know who created the station.

> *A vision is a medium of exchange because it is transferable.*

If no other person can run with the vision except the visionary, it is not a vision. If a vision is not transferable, it is just an idea or concept. Ideas and concepts do not have to be transferable to be successful; however, visions do. Allow me to illustrate. A very successful entrepreneur created a machine that could make plastic tanks for collecting rain or mains water. There is a real need for such a device in the Islands because water is a scarce commodity. So this entrepreneur set up factories throughout the Islands to manufacture these tanks and become very successful. His idea or concept was the machine, but the factory all around the Islands was the vision. The idea or concept did not need to be transferable to be successful; in fact, if it were the business, it would fail because many other people would duplicate the machine. However, the vision had to be transferable to be successful. Thus this man found partners around the Islands who would run with his vision. If the vision could not be transferred, this business would not work because nobody can run with it. There are many people with good ideas or concepts of how to improve or better things, but these ideas or concepts do not necessarily translate into a successful vision. How many times have people come and shared good ideas or concepts with you, but it never translates into a successful vision? It happens all the time.

For a vision to be transferable, it must accomplish three things. First, it must meet a need. Someone came up with a philosophy that said, "find a need and fill it." A vision must meet a need before it can become transferable material. It must answer a problem that generally every person in that community is experiencing. *Second, a vision must be relevant.* People and problems change over time, and if your vision is not relevant to their current situation, nobody can identify with it. Someone else said, "there is nothing more powerful than an idea whose time has come." *Third, a vision must be quantifiable.* Can some number or statistic be put to it, or is it merely just theoretical. It is challenging to get people to run with theories or hypothesis because it is not quantifiable. People want to know how much it is going to cost. Every recipient of the vision has a right to expect these three questions to be answered before running with the vision. If the recipient cannot see a need being answered by your vision, they will not be interested. If they cannot see the relevance in your vision, they will not be compelled to run with it, and if they cannot put a number to it, they will not know how to support it.

Can the vision be documented?

> For a vision to be transferable, it must accomplish three things. First, it must meet a need. Second, a vision must be relevant. Third, a vision must be quantifiable.

I come from a culture where our roots date back to a thousand years before Christ. Everything that was handed down from our ancestors had to be verbalized in some form of chant, song, or story before it could be passed on to succeeding generations. Our culture is an oral culture. Therefore, much of what happened in our prehistory is unknown because oral traditions are never as detailed as written traditions. However, when the early missionaries and explorers came to the Pacific Islands, one of the things they did was to document in writing many of these stories and what generally was happening at the time. Today these records are an invaluable and rich source of scholarship for many cultural anthropologists and historians studying our world's region. *A vision must be documentable to be a vision. When it cannot be documented, then it is merely a story.* The problem with stories is that they can be changed or manipulated in so many different ways. I have been a recipient of stories, and I am sure you have been too, that have been changed or manipulated, so by the time it reached my ears, it is so different from what actually happened. I received a call from a companion who said that he heard a story that a good friend of mine was dead. This was an absolute shock to me, so I decided to ring up this friend, and behold, he answers the phone. I later found out that the person who had died was a companion of my friend. If you could have been there to see my reaction, you would understand the joy I felt knowing that my friend was alive.

Documenting the vision does three things for the vision. Firstly, it puts a FRAMEWORK to the vision. It is what I call FRAMING the vision.

> *A vision must be documentable to be a vision. When it cannot be documented, then it is merely a story.*

The vision will have a tangible picture that people can see and meditate on. People will grasp and receive its idea or concepts because they see what you are saying. They have a framework before their eyes and ears. *Secondly, it puts a VALUE to the vision. I call this VALUATING the vision.* If people cannot see your vision, they cannot make a value judgment about what you are saying. People are moved to act when the question of value is answered. A Pastor once said to me, "if you want to succeed at anything, put a value to it!" What people cannot see or hear cannot be valued, and what cannot be valued cannot be received. *Third, it puts an AUTHORITY to the vision. I call this AUTHORIZING the vision.* It is like striking a seal of authority on a document. When that seal appears on the document, you know it has the authority of whatever person or organization is behind that seal. When the vision becomes written material, it becomes authorized. As long as the vision is undocumented, it is subject to all kinds of changes, and it is questionable. People are more apt to believe and accept what is written down than what is verbal. In fact, oral statements are simply unreliable because of their very nature being verbal. Please write it down, and people will take notice of it. A note of warning after documenting the vision, do not share it openly with people but be selective with people with who you share it.

> Documenting the vision does three things for the vision. Firstly, it puts a FRAMEWORK to the vision. Secondly, it puts a VALUE to the vision. Thirdly, it puts an AUTHORITY to the vision.

I have received and accomplished many grand visions in my years and continue to do so. I had learned that I was taking what I had seen and received to another level when I began documenting these visions. *When you document a vision, you remove it from the realm of the unseen to the realm of the seen.* We can term this process as transubstantiating your vision. Transubstantiation means to change the substance of something into another form. When a vision is in a mental state, it is merely in the unseen realm, in the form of pictures in our mind, but when it is written down, it becomes substance meaning it can be evidenced; therefore, it is capable of being fulfilled. As long as a vision remains undocumented, nothing would ever happen to it, and it will stay at that level for the rest of its life and will probably die when the visionary dies, and no one will ever know that this visionary had the vision first. When you read through the annals of prehistory, you quickly discover that many ideas and concepts we thought were invented in our generation were first used by primitive cultures thousands of years before, but because it was not documented, we cannot say for sure. For example, the ancient Inca Indians of South America have primitive pictures of hang gliders on their pottery; therefore, some scientists believe they were the first to fly and not the Wright brothers of America!

Can the vision be adapted?

> *Vision must be adaptable. When environmental factors change, we must adapt the vision but not change the vision.*

Vision must be adaptable. A vision is a living thing; it will change. Often what you start off with is not the same thing you will end up with, and sometimes what you end up with is not the same thing as what you started with. It can be bigger or smaller than what you had initially anticipated. There is no way of telling what will happen with the vision, despite our best estimates or predictions. Therefore we must allow for change because the vision's environment is always subject to change. A change of environment can either contract or expand the vision. *When environmental factors change, we must adapt the vision but not change the vision.* Environmental factors should never change the vision. If the vision is changed due to a change in the environment, then it is a new vision but not an adapted vision.

Five environmental factors can cause adaptation to vision.

1 The people factor.

2 The economic factor.

3 The social factor.

4 The bureaucratic factor.

5 The political factor.

Let us briefly look at how each of these factors can cause a vision to adapt. I will use an illustrated story to demonstrate its effect upon a vision. For example, the vision is to build a family soup restaurant called Hot Pot, specializing in making and selling all sorts of soups. We will call the visionary Ben.

The people factor

The dream started with Ben's grandmother, who made terrific soups when Ben was a young man. One day Ben had a vision of taking his grandmother's soup recipes and turning them into a restaurant business. So he wrote out this vision of a restaurant using his grandmother's recipes, and Ben was banking on his grandmother to help him start the restaurant. The only problem is Ben's grandmother died suddenly, and she did not teach Ben how to cook these soups, and Ben's mother never took a liking to it. Ben has all these recipes with him, but no one knows how to cook these beautiful soups. Ben has a human resource problem, so the vision calls for an adaptation. Ben has several options, such as to hire a cook or experiment himself and learn, or he can ask around the family if anyone knows how to cook grandma's soups. He decided to discover himself. After several months of testing, he masters His grandmother's soups.

The economic factor

Ben later finds a partner to help him with the business by bringing in some of the capital he will need to set up the business. So he and his partner cost out the vision, and it was going to cost them 60,000 dollars to start the business. But two things happened in the meantime that threatens to increase this cost to 90,000 dollars. The space Ben was counting on renting for the restaurant is taken out, and only a more expensive venue is available uptown. The tourist industry has taken a slump because of an increase in the value of the dollar. Ben has an economic problem, which calls for an adaptation. Ben has several options; he can wait for the situation to improve or find another partner to make up the excess or borrow the rest from the bank. He decides to borrow the rest and move uptown. The risk factor has increased, but the potential of the vision remains the same.

The social factor

The new area in which Ben now wants to set up this restaurant has all sorts of high profile restaurants in it because of the cliental in this area. This is a very upmarket area, and people here like classy and expensive food. Ben is unsure if they will like the taste of his soups and the concept of his family soup restaurant. Ben has a social problem that calls for an adaptation. Ben has several options; he can add to his menu soup for classy people or create a new trend in this area or increase his menu by adding other side dishes to compliment his soup. Ben decides to do all three.

The bureaucratic factor

Ben then applies for a business license, but he finds out that the local area council will not allow any more restaurant business's to be started in this area. Ben has a bureaucratic problem that calls for an adaptation. However, he finds out that a restaurant can only be allowed under the condition that it is part of a gift shop selling local artifacts for tourists because that is what the council wants to see in this area. Ben has several options; he can take them to court for unfair practice or wait for space somewhere else or take up the additional challenge. He decides to take up the extra challenge.

The political factor

Two of the restaurant owners in the area are threatened by Ben's vision, so they go and see the Mayor about it and tell him that if he can influence the council not to issue Ben a license, they promise the Mayor that they will financially support him in the upcoming elections. The council informs Ben that his license is on hold but offers him no plausible explanation. Ben has a political problem that calls for an adaptation. A council member tells Ben that the problem is the Mayor and these two opposing restaurant owners. Ben has several options; he can take up the matter with his parliament member or go to court or campaign against the existing Mayor and hope for his opponent to win in an upcoming election. Ben decided to campaign against the current Mayor. The Mayor's opponent wins, and Ben finds himself hosting the mayor and the council at his grand opening.

Some concluding thoughts

In each of these situations, the vision was forced to adapt by circumstances beyond Ben's control. What started as a vision for a simple family soup restaurant ended up as a high-class soup family restaurant with a gift shop and the best customers in town? If a vision fails to adapt, it will die. Ben recognized the importance of flexibility in a vision. A vision is flexible when it is adaptable. Some people prefer to call these factors as "struggles in birthing your vision." I agree, but unless we face these situations with a flexible mindset, these struggles will undoubtedly be the very thing that will kill your vision. It happens all the time. A flexible mindset will accept these factors as "stepping stones" to achieving the vision rather than problems against the vision. As a rule, don't try and change the circumstances but change your approach! This is basically how Ben saw these situations. Because of his flexible mindset, he was able to adapt and overcome every obstacle as a stepping stone to fulfilling his vision, and as a result, things turned out a lot better than he had expected. I like the way a very successful entrepreneur put it; he said, "Every setback is a setup for a comeback!"

I have a good friend who now lives in Australia. Many years ago, he shared with me his vision to become an airline pilot. So he packed up his family and left for Australia to pursue this vision. He was prepared to pay the cost and put in the hours to qualify for his pilot's license. However, on taking a medical check-up, it was discovered that he was partly color blind, meaning he could only see a certain range of colors; therefore, he was disqualified from flying. Most people would have given up at this stage, but my friend saw a way he could adapt his vision. So he decided to become an aircraft mechanic, which is, of course, is a much harder profession to qualify. He is now a qualified 747 mechanic earning as much as a 747 captain with all the same Company benefits, and best of all, he gets to test all of the planes while they are on the ground! Essentially my friend achieved his vision because he was prepared to adapt his vision.

Inspiration refers to those visions that come directly from GOD/UNIVERSE.

CHAPTER FIVE

The Nature of Vision

The nature of vision is those attributes of vision that allow a vision to be shared or passed on to others. For instance, how can a person who is not a visionary become a visionary, or how can a person who is not a visionary receive a vision? There are primarily three ways a person can become a visionary or receive a vision.

1 BY INSPIRATION.

2 BY ASSOCIATION.

3 BY OBSERVATION.

4 BY DECREE.

By *Inspiration*

Inspiration refers to visions that come directly from GOD/UNIVERSE. I have already spoken about the GOD/UNIVERSE factor in vision. Still, at this point, I would like to explain how vision can come by inspiration from GOD/UNIVERSE, and I am mindful you may be an agnostic or an atheist, so please hear me out. There are primarily three ways that a vision can be channeled to you from GOD/UNIVERSE. First, through thoughts or impressions upon your mind. Second, through dreams or trances while unconscious. Third, through an audible voice, you hear whether the source is invisible or visible, like an angelic visitation. Personally, I have not received any vision through an audible voice, but I know of many Godly people who claim they have received their visions from an audible voice. In fact, most of the founders of the major religions of this World claim an audible voice as the source of their writings (visions). Some even claim that angels spoke to them audibly, giving them the vision. While this is rather an uncommon method, it never the less does occur. Most of the visions I have received have been through impressions on my mind or trances I have had while entirely conscious. The point here is not to go looking for inspiration but be open to inspiration when they come in their own time. If you are uncertain about the vision, give it a time or wait for confirmation from other people.

> *Inspiration refers to those visions that come directly from GOD/UNIVERSE.*

Most of the visions I have received I know never came from me. The reason I know this is because I know my limitations and my abilities. If it were left to me, I would never have come up with some of these visions. Some of you are already identifying with what I am saying because some of those visions you have received were so grand, or they came at such a crucial time or were so fitting to the situation that you know it was not from you; therefore, they are inspirations from GOD/UNIVERSE. I have a friend who resigned from his job to run with a vision he believed was from GOD. Without a job, he was down to his last dollar, but because he believed that his vision was from GOD, he persevered through many trials to see his vision completed. Seven years later, he now sits in a 20 million dollar building and owns a brand new house and car. The last time I met him, he talked to me about a vision that GOD had given him an airplane, which I have no doubt he will achieve soon. If you are agnostic or an atheist, I respect your position, but I ask that you be open to the possibility that a higher force is behind the vision or consider this other way.

By *Association*

Vision can also come by association. Association means being joined to another for a common purpose. If a person who lacks vision continuously associates with a person of vision, that person will also become a visionary in due time or at the least receive a vision. What I mean by association is not some sort of casual or social meetings where you meet your peers or friends to have a relaxed time of fellowship every week. What I mean is continuously associating yourself with that visionary. Becoming a part of what the visionary does by working for or being schooled under the visionary operation or ministry. Take, for example, a very successful executive business manager who is a visionary. He is the CEO of a top multinational food Company, and because he is a person of vision, the Company is always ahead of the competition. If, say, Ben, before he became a restaurant owner and was not a visionary, became a part of this man's working team and continuously associated himself with this person, Ben too will in time become a business visionary or at least catch a vision from this man. Many visionaries of today, if they are honest, will tell you that someone or persons influenced them in their visionary direction. It is very rare to find a person that was born a visionary; the majority of people become visionaries or catch vision through association. Someone said, "We do not discover champions; we make them." It is the same with visionaries; we do not discover them; we make them.

> *Vision can also come by association. Association means being joined to another for a common purpose.*

In our television ministry, every time we needed a new video editor or cameraman, we would put out an advertisement for fresh school leavers. We rarely took on professional people because we understood that it is easier to give untrained people vision. Most of the people who applied had no experience in this field, and some had no computing skills. We understood the risk. But by the time they graduated with us, they were experts and had excelled beyond many professional people in the television industry in my country. We never gave them the gift or talent; they always had it with them. We merely helped them to discover it and build on it through vision by association. Today some of these individuals have moved on and are being used by other people to fulfill their vision. We are blessed to hear how many of these people we trained have become leaders in their field. It is essential to understand that there is a timeframe to become a visionary or to receive a vision. It can take anywhere from one year to ten years. There are simply no shortcuts to this process. It all hinges on the character and the commitment of the individual and the commitment and character of the person who imparts vision to you. There must be a good connection before there is impartation!

By *Observation*

We have in our little country certain families whose profession is passed on from one generation to the next generation. For example, the dad was a doctor, so the son becomes a doctor, and his son or daughter is in medical school studying to be a doctor. This is very prevalent in the area of Church ministry in my country, where we have families who have four to five generations of pastors. I am sure the same thing happens in your own communities. This is not an accident or a coincidence. *We also acquire vision by observation.* What we observe as children, as teenagers as young adults will affect us. You cannot observe something all your life and not have it influence you. Eventually, it gets into your subconscious, and it becomes a part of your being. Whatever profession is in the family, it is very likely will be the children's profession. That is why many parents desiring their children to take on or over their profession involve their children at a young age in what they do. My father had a desire for me to become a lawyer, but he was not a lawyer but thinks like a lawyer, so he would often lecture me about the advantages of being a lawyer, and he would often refer to a successful lawyer, a friend of his as a model of who he wanted me to be. What my father was doing was schooling me into his dream. So he sent me to an expensive private school to realize this end. I managed to get into university, where I completed my degrees but not in the law area; although I was partway there, I had to abruptly finish my studies because my father fell ill and I had to return home. I had only two and half more years to complete to finish a law degree.

> *We also acquire vision by observation. Observation means intently looking and then studying what is observed with the purpose of changing or improving it.*

I do not ever regret not going back to complete my law studies because the visionary gift that my father had is to me more important than receiving a Ph.D. in law. However, not everyone who is raised up in a family where there is a strong pull towards some particular profession will take on the family profession. In fact, in most cases, there is no family profession at all. Therefore, most people get vision through observing a need and being moved to fill that need. I have already touched on this as a property of visions, so let me briefly define what observation means as it applies to vision. *Observation means intently looking and then studying what is observed with the purpose of changing or improving it.* Vision comes as the answer to what is observed. The Islands of Fiji hit the worldwide media attention in 1987 when an Army Kernel named Rambuka Sitivini, a native-born Fijian, lead the first national Coup to overthrown a legitimately nationally elected Fijian government lead by an Indian PM and Indian majority. Nothing like this had ever happened in Fiji before, and people were in shock. However, we here in the Islands knew precisely why it had happened. Kernel Rambuka knew that if native Fijians did not rise up and do something about the growing economic and political power of the introduced Indian population, native Fijians would eventually lose their lands and rights. Kernel Rambuka observed the need and had the vision to do something about it. Later generations may call him a tyrant or a hero, but I prefer to call him a visionary.

By *Decree*

Finally, vision can also come by decree. By Decree means a power or force beyond this earthly realm has determined the vision; therefore, the outcome is certain. I have avoided quoting the Bible in this book until now. Have you noticed that whenever the nation of Israel was in a crisis, GOD sent a vision to deliver or save his people, usually from an enemy? Notice GOD did not send a great army, powerful weapons to defeat their enemies, or a chest of gold to buy their way out of it. He sent a man, usually a prophet, with a vision. We preacher calls it "a Word." Take, for example, Moses; GOD spoke to Moses. He said to Moses, "Go to Pharaoh and say to him, 'This is what YHWH, the GOD of the Hebrews, says: "Let my people go, so that they may worship me." In the next few passages, GOD explained to Moses precisely what He intended to do (Exodus 9).

The vision came by way of a decree. Moses had a choice to run with the decree (the vision) or run from it. The rest we know is history. Moses's name lives in infinity because he obeyed. Time after time, when Israel disobeyed YHWH, and their enemies defeated them only to repent and cry out to YHWH for mercy. In response, the pattern was always the same. He sent the vision by way of a decree to deliver and save them. The result is already determined. This aspect of vision is by no means exclusive to the Bible. Many people in different religions profess to receive decrees from Heaven and have seen the result of their vision. This is not a common way, but it happens when GOD/UNIVERSE determines He wants something done on Earth.

> *By Decree means a power or force beyond this earthly realm has determined the vision; therefore, the outcome is certain.*

Mahatma Gandhi was an extraordinary man, a Moses of his time. Gandhi was a devout Hindu who studied and respected the beliefs of other religions and practiced austere fasting. He lived a life of a vegetarian, believing it was wrong to kills animals. Before Gandhi was ever inducted into the hall of fame of the righteous of humanity, He was a man who was broken and listened to GOD. From his youth, he was devoted to prayer and fasting. We know him from our history books as an Indian lawyer, anti-colonial nationalist, and political ethicist who employed nonviolent resistance to lead the successful campaign for India's independence from British rule in 1947 and inspired movements for civil rights and freedom across the world. Gandhi's political activism began in South Africa, where he faced tremendous discrimination and abuse. It was there that he developed his political views, ethics, and politics, specifically the methodology of Satyagraha (devotion to the truth), or nonviolent protest the first time. Gandhi battled against the forces of discrimination and violence in South Africa for two decades. When he moved back to India in 1915, He brought an international reputation as a leading Indian nationalist, theorist, and community organizer. He returned to India with a decree for her independence from British rule. He has heard from GOD, and there was no stopping him. He knew he was GOD's decree. I quote, "My aspiration is limited. God has not given me the power to guide the world on the path of non-violence. But I have imagined that He has chosen me as His instrument for presenting non-violence to India for dealing with her many ills. The progress already made is great. But much more remains to be done." He summarized his decree in these words; "It is through truth & non-violence that I can have some glimpse of God. Truth & non-violence are my God. They are the obverse and reverse of the same coin."

Some concluding thoughts

Some of you may have asked at some point, is not vision something we are all born with, or maybe it is a gift from GOD/UNIVERSE? To answer this question, we need to understand the difference between a vision and "the capacity of vision." I believe we are all born with the "innate" (inborn) capacity to receive a vision or dream, but visions do not come just because we have this "endowed" capacity. You will be surprised at the number of people who don't even have a vision or let alone dream a dream. Vision of itself is independent of this capacity because no one can put a patent, a pattern, or claim ownership of the capacity to dream or visualize, but we can patent or patent a vision once it is verified as being completely original. Therefore, I don't believe that the capacity of vision is a gift because everyone has this capacity to receive visions. Still, I do believe that visions are a gift from GOD/UNIVERSE if you believe that vision can come by inspiration. I have met many people who have been at the bottom of a situation and have confessed to me that they recovered from their position because they received a vision, giving them direction, which they know did not originate with them. Without this capacity to receive visions, these people would have lost hope.

The critical point here is developing this innate capacity we have been endowed with to receive more visions readily. To do this, we must be prepared to let go of our fears, preconceived ideas, cultural and traditional limitations, and those parts of our education or training that have stunted this capacity. Specifically, factors that create "mindsets" in us that limit the process of vision. A mindset is a mental stronghold, which could be a belief, a value, or a taboo that we have accepted that prevents us from stepping out and beyond. Some of you reading this book could well be facing some difficult situation you do not know how to overcome. Still, you are being prevented from your very solution because of a particular mindset. Well, I have some excellent news for you! Visions more often come as answers to uncertainties, problems, or tragedies that we are facing. They give us direction, hope, and faith to move forward under all conditions, and if you are prepared today to move beyond that mindset, you will see it come to pass. However, there is a definite process that many people do not understand about bringing vision into a pass, which I would like to share with you now.

VPOWER

How do you know when you have a vision? It is very simple; it consumes your thoughts and preoccupies your time. When something consumes you, it captivates you.

CHAPTER SIX

The Process of Vision

A process is a course of action and reaction to realizing the end of a thing. Vision has a process of realization that, if not understood, would cause frustration and unfruitfulness. There are six stages in the process of realizing a vision, as illustrated in the following flow chart.

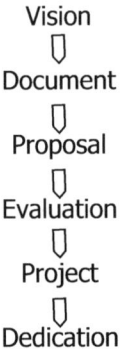

We will examine these stages individually to allow you to see how simple the process of realizing a vision can be.

Vision

By now, we should understand what vision is and how important it is to have a vision. This is the first and most crucial stage in the process of realizing vision is to have a vision. A famous psychologist said, "Beginning is half done." *How do you know when you have a vision? It is very simple; it consumes your thoughts and preoccupies your time. When something consumes you, it captivates you. When vision comes, you cannot stop thinking about it and meditating on it.* You roll it from the left side of your brain to the right side of your brain until your brain is sore from its rocking motion. When something preoccupies you, it costs you something. It will cost you sleep time as you reflect upon it past the midnight hour, and it will cost you money as you search for some preliminary facts to establish that it is genuine. Once the vision comes, it will not let go of you no matter what you try to do to resist its power. A genuine vision will always uplift your soul and excite your being. Vision never creates a feeling of despair or hopelessness. It is like a light in a dark tunnel. It is the moon in a pitch dark night. I also like to view this process of vision as becoming impregnated by the sperm of hope. After you are impregnated with hope, like a woman in labor, it will take nine months for her to give birth to her baby. It is the same with vision; it will take time to give birth to the vision. Like labor pains, there will be struggles along the way, times where you feel like giving up, running away, but all become relatively insignificant when you give birth to it.

Document

> *How do you know when you have a vision? It is very simple; it consumes your thoughts and preoccupies your time. When something consumes you, it captivates you.*

During the time when the mother is carrying the baby, many couples will go to a doctor to have the baby scanned or x-rayed. It is at this point the couple comes to learn the sex of their child and many other important details about their child. This is like documenting the vision before it gives birth. We have already discussed this phase in detail; therefore, it is sufficient to remind you *that you need to proceed to document it once the vision is conceived*. It is at this stage we come to learn many things about the vision that may not have been clear at the start when we first received it. Perhaps its purpose or some other property of the vision was not clear, but when you documented it, it became rather apparent. In a sense, it is like putting a jigsaw puzzle together. When you start off, you have a picture in your mind of what the thing looks like. But as you put it down on paper, it starts to flow, and it starts to make sense. People that you had casually described your vision to that were unsure or unclear after reading it will exclaim, "I see it now yes it makes perfect sense!" *While the vision remains unwritten, expect people to be unclear and uncertain about what you are saying.*

Proposal

A proposal is a tool that a financial analyst or marketer uses to get people interested in implementing a vision. *It is a very fancy report that details many facts and factors that people will naturally ask about the vision.* It has two parts to it called; the business proposal and the business plan. For that reason, it is often ten times the size of your documented vision and is prepared by a professional accountant or consultant. A proposal can cost anywhere from 1 to 5 percent of the vision's total cost, hence why many people do not progress to this stage, but there are ways of minimizing this cost. For example, making the accountant or consultant a part of the vision, i.e., giving them a slice of the cake or perhaps negotiating a fixed or a conditional fee. Finding a friend in this area who can do it on credit for you or find an organization that could provide preliminary funding, like a grant or gift, etc.

> *Once the vision is conceived, you need to proceed to document it. While the vision remains unwritten, expect people to be unclear and uncertain about what you are saying.*

The proposal will contain an overview of your vision, including your concepts, ideas, and principles. It will spell out your goals, objectives, and plan to realize the vision. It will list all the necessary labor sources, materials, and equipment that the vision will need. It will also show all the products, benefits, and services that your vision will create. Attached to this will be a comprehensive analyst of costs, expenditures, and profit, if applicable. A proposal puts a face of professionalism and excellence on your vision to dispel the natural fears that people will have about your vision. But first, unless these facts convince you, it will certainly not impact others. It would be worthwhile at this stage to have other people whom you can trust brainstorm or critique your vision before going to the next level. This will help "polish" the proposal before going to the sources. Once the proposal is completed, it must then go through an evaluation stage.

Evaluation

> *A proposal is a very fancy report that details many facts and factors that people will naturally ask about the vision.*

This is where the proposal is then tabled with possible or eligible sources to fund the vision. Evaluation is the most challenging stage of the vision because it demands patients and understanding. Prospects and Authorities will want time to evaluate the proposal and will most likely have questions they perceive are problems or barriers with the proposal. This is where frustration or anger can set in, especially when time is considered, or some factors like labor or council approvals are critical to the proposal. The most important thing to realize about the evaluation stage is not every organization or institution that evaluates your proposal will be as enthusiastic or convinced about it. It will take time for people to see and believe in what you are proposing. This, of course, will all depend on how well your proposal has been researched and prepared. It is not unusual to have proposals rejected two or three times before it is finally accepted or a proposal to be passed through several sources for consideration before the right source is found. It is all about connecting the vision to the right people. I have known of proposals that have been accepted within a few days of its presentation, others months, and still other years. The most important thing here is not to lose hope while waiting but to continue to believe in the best.

Project

> *Evaluation is where the proposal is then tabled with possible or eligible sources to fund the vision.*

Perhaps this is the most exciting stage of the vision when it becomes a project. This is the implementation stage. This is when it goes out to the architects, builders, and whoever else is involved in the construction phase to submit quotes and costs to build the project. *This is when all the fine details are sorted out and cost out, and timing is decided.* There is a lot of paperwork involved at this stage because structure and organization are essential to the implementation stage. At this stage, a project manager needs to be appointed, and it is most often the visionary himself or herself who takes on this position. As I mentioned earlier, most visionaries find it difficult to relinquish this phase to another person because no other person will have the passion, commitment, and understanding that the visionary will have. This is also the stage where things will go wrong and will need adjustments. I spoke about how a vision will require adaptation as reality meets vision. The vision does not get changed, but it adapts itself to the circumstances. As I have said, even the best assumptions, predictions, and projections can be wrong, and the project can turn out to be more expensive or much cheaper, and time can be shorter or longer. But if you will tarry and not give up, it shall surely come to pass.

Dedication

> *Project is when all the fine details are sorted out and cost out, and timing is decided.*

I have attended many dedication ceremonies, some small, some big, and I am sure you have too. This is when the project is completed and is to be commissioned. There are many emotions involved at this stage because the people who have built the project have been under pressure and come under fire, and to see it all complete and finally dedicated is an overwhelming thing. At this stage, acknowledgments and presentations are made to honor those who have been involved in the project. There are a variety of ways people dedicate their visions and honor those involved. This is something that is open to the culture, custom, or tradition of the respective ethos. Dedication is also a time of celebration and feasting. *The important factor about dedication is that it officially marks the end of the vision.*

The vision may not have turned out perfect or faultless, but it never marks the end of the vision. What we do after this is like

> *The important factor about dedication is that it officially marks the end of the vision.*

nursing an infant who has been born. This has to do with the maturing or development phase, which is outside our discussion scope. It would be best if you remembered that while dedication may mark the end of the vision, it is also at this stage that new visions start to emerge. The vision to expand what you have achieved to other areas, cities, or countries.

Some concluding thoughts

The process of vision is a metamorphosis activity. The word metamorphosis means to change into another form. This word metamorphosis is derived from the process that we see in nature when a caterpillar is transformed into a butterfly. It never ceases to amaze me how a grotesque and ugly-looking thing like a caterpillar gets transformed into a dazzling beautiful butterfly. In a sense, this is what happens to vision as it undergoes and completes its process. People are often never dazzled or impressed by the vision when they first learn of it or read it, but they are absolutely amazed when they finally see it. Very often, it is the visionary who is more surprised than anyone else! And for those visions that did not turn out in the way that you may have expected. Remember, what you see at the end is not what will be in the future. There is a process of maturing the vision that can take anywhere from one to ten years. It is during this time that the vision grows into or changes to become what you initially saw. It is often the shell we start with, and the rest will be filled in as time passes.

When a vision is fantasy-centered, it will be unpractical; in other words, it is in the realm of imagination.

CHAPTER SEVEN

The Pitfalls of Vision

A pitfall can be defined as a barrier or a stumbling block that can cause a vision to go off course or stop in its track. A pitfall can never destroy a vision but can only impair or delay its ultimate fulfillment. A vision will always find its fulfillment despite the pitfalls. While it is not possible to document every potential pitfall that can plague or delay a vision's fulfillment, there are pitfalls common to any vision that can be constructively avoided. These common barriers can surface before, during, or after the vision has been implemented, and they can surface at any stage in the process of vision. It is important to remember that these are only temporary impairments that are never meant to be permanent blockages. Therefore, we should not give up or abandon the vision because, in its time, a vision will always find another way to fulfill itself, which has to do with the vices of a vision that will be dealt with in the next chapter. Here are some of those pitfalls and their objective examples.

Undercapitalized visions

> *A pitfall can be defined as a barrier or a stumbling block that can cause a vision to go off course or stop in its track.*

For a vision to be effective and productive, it must have the right injection of resources. For some visions, it will be the suitable building and location; for others, it will be the right labor skills or work experience, others the right technology or the right know-how, etc. All of which has a financial cost to it, which is called the capital needed to start the vision. Many business ventures fail in the first or second year of their operation because they had inadequate resources to start it off and sustain it. Consequently, it has become a standard practice in preparing proposals to budget in your first year's expenses while you build the vision. Most banks that lend money for new business ventures allow for this because they know from experience that this is a common problem, why many business ventures fail. The reality is it takes time to build up the vision, i.e., the support for its continued success and growth.

A man in my country, which I will call Mr. Peters, started a new television station. Mr. Peter's vision was unique in that he offered programming of which was new to the local populace. His business proposal and plan showed that he would be successful. His business proposal showed that he had the industry experience, being a former manager of another television station; he had secured the rights to the best programs from overseas and had several experienced people who would work for him. Mr. Peters leased a channel and building from another local television operator to start his venture and obtained a small loan to start his operation. From the onset of his launch, he began to experience operational problems that are typical of an undercapitalized vision. He could not afford to purchase the right equipment, pay the programs he obtained the rights for, nor could he afford to pay the people he hired. After three months of starting, Mr. Peters ran out of money, and the used equipment he obtained in the lease was causing him problems because it could not do what he envisioned the station to be. Mr. Peters shut shop after one year of his launch. Yet many knew this man had a great vision and the talent and experience to achieve his vision, but his vision failed because of undercapitalization.

Under skilled visions

> *For a vision to be effective and productive, it must have the right injection of resources.*

Skill is a commodity that takes years to build and perfect. Therefore, skilled people come at a price, and the rarer and or more productive they are, the more costly it will be to fulfilling your vision. Even if the visionary possessed all the skills he or she requires to build the vision, sooner or later, that skill has to be passed on to someone that can build or carry on the vision. Training people to the level of skill required to run the vision takes time and money. *Many visions temporally fail because of under-skilled or wrongly skilled people.* The inability to produce, compete or excel in your vision can cause the vision to fail temporally. Consequently, every project, whether it is a business venture or a particular field of pursuit, invests resources in equipping themselves or their people with the right skills and knowledge for their project.

I once hired a man; I will call Jim to help me build my vision for a Media Communication Centre who turned out to be a disaster in the making because he simply could not do the job. Jim lacked the skill and the ability to do his tasks because of inexperience, and because he had a physical problem, he was overweight and sedentary. My choice of him was motivated by the fact that Jim was an honest man and he had a qualification in an area of my vision, where that type of skill was often employed. Although Jim was faithful and committed at his job and could do most of the tasks, he could not perform the task in areas where it was vital to maintain my vision. Consequently, an equipment accident occurred, which cost me several hundreds of thousands because he took a risk in a task where caution should have been exercised, and he almost killed a worker. In the end, Jim resigned, and I suffered loss because he was un-skilled for my vision. I understand I was partly to blame; my desire to help him and his family made my error.

I centered visions. Another pitfall that people often do with vision is to build the vision on them and not on its purpose. Consequently, when that person leaves

> *Many visions temporally fail because of under-skilled or wrongly skilled people.*

the organization or dies, the entity they created falls apart or starts to fade into oblivion because the vision was built on them as a person. While some visions may be unique to the person, especially if the person has a unique ability or gift, making that vision non-transferable to someone else. Never the less it will be a mistake to build that vision on your individuality and ability because the fact is we are all expendable and expiable. For that reason, the vision should be built around something that is durable, which can carry the vision beyond a specific expiry date. In other words, when you are unable to continue your vision on, or you die, the vision will still carry on through some other vehicle that you created that is independent of you. Many use vehicles such as a Trust, a Foundation, a Company or a Charity, etc.

I remember a very successful organization that operated in my country, which I will call Mission Impossible (MI). The organization's members multiplied under the leadership of a charismatic man whom I will call Tom. When Tom left, MI fell from prominence to insignificance because Tom cleverly built MI on himself. So when Tom left, he took most of its followers. The organization had a very powerful vision and was doing much good in my country, but through the leadership ability of Tom, he was able to usurp the vision of the organization and skillfully centre it on himself. Tom did it through skilled diplomacy and deception, which caught the organization off guard because they had not seen what had happened until it was too late. Tom had created an I-centered vision and almost destroyed the organization because its board was not aware of the pitfall of the building I-centered visions. When this man left the organization, nearly all of its members flowed him.

Fantasy-based visions

> Another pitfall that people often do with vision is to build the vision on them and not on its purpose.

When a vision is fantasy-based, it will be unpractical; in other words, it is in the realm of imagination. People often get confused with an infatuation or inspiration of which are not visions but are illusions of grandeur or greatness that are not grounded to the reality of the real world they live in. The imagination is a vital part of developing a vision. Still, when it becomes a journey into the unreal and unknown, they are no longer a vision but an explicit fantasy. Fantasy can never be translated into a vision because of its impossible and impractical conditions. Some people like to call these specific situation dreams and term the people who come up with these dreams "dreamers" which are a miss-representation of what is a dreamer really is. See Chapter two. A dream becomes a vision when it can be translated into a practical and workable project.

Not so long ago, I met a man who had a vision of a communication system that would cover the world. I will call him Harry. Harry's vision was well documented and well supported with the right research and models. The only pitfall it had was that it would cost over seven billion Eurodollars to fund the project. Harry had approached many sources to solicit funding, but they all rejected the project. The sources did not question the communication system's ability to deliver what it was designed to do or question the benefits of what the financial plan promised to do. Still, they rejected Harry's project because the funding he was asking for was simply out of the reach of any financial institution that lent monies for these types of projects. In other words, this project was in the fantasy zone and may never be realized because of that one reason.

Un-futured visions

A successful motivational speaker said, "That success without a successor is a failure." By the same tone, a vision that does not have a successor will not have a future. *While it is quite conceivable that a vision may have a short-term outlook, it is never without a long-term outlook.* After they have long gone from this world, every visionary would like to see their vision impacting generations to come, and indeed is the dream of most visionaries. Many visionaries make the mistake of placing their vision into the hand of a person who has not run with the visionary or worked with the visionary because they will not have the visionary's heart for the vision. After a few years of its implementation, I have seen visions crash because the visionary chose the wrong person to take on the vision's future.

> *When a vision is fantasy-based, it will be unpractical; in other words, it is in the realm of imagination.*

A very successful wholesaler in my town hired a manager whom I will call Thomas to run their family business. For many years, the family business led in this market because it was a long-standing business in my country. Thomas knew nothing about the vision and the heart of the Company's founder since he never spent any time with its founder. Thomas did not have the character and intuition of the business founder; he was a novice. He did not understand the sacrifices and pains that the founder of that business went through to be where they were. Thomas chartered a course for the business that assumed risks and debts beyond the business's ability to handle, which its founder would never have allowed. As a result, the company went into financial trouble, so they fired the manager, but it was too late to save the Company. This man was an example of an un-futured vision.

Un-chartered visions

> *While it is quite conceivable that a vision may have a short-term outlook, it is never without a long-term outlook.*

It is one matter to document the vision; it is another matter to chart the vision's course. *The fact is many visions end up in un-chartered waters because they failed to chart a proper course for their vision.* This has to do with the short-term and long-term position and direction of the vision. Where do you see this vision at, at some defined period in the future? It should have realistic, quantified, and time-based aims and goals for every year as you progress through its gradual fulfillment. The details of this should be in your project proposal. However, what is essential here is knowing and understanding the overall course of where the vision is heading. A vision needs to be chartered to make sure it achieves its intended purpose. I have mentioned that often circumstances require us to adapt the vision, but these circumstances should never change the vision if it has a known and charted course.

A very well-qualified architect in my country started an architect business of whom I will call Andrew. Andrew's business soon became the leading architectural firm and was awarded many prestigious projects to design and manage. Most of the huge infrastructure and building projects were designed by Andrew's firm. However, problems started to occur with Andrew's vision when he took the business into unchartered territory. Andrew started to build the buildings and structures he designed, which was not part of the vision in the beginning. He entered into an unchartered territory where he had no past experience and proven strength. Many building firms were experienced and proven in this domain, working in this area for many years, some of which were branches of giant international corporations. As an architect, Andrew was unbeatable because this is where the strength of his vision laid, but as a builder, he was most vulnerable, and consequently, he lost millions through his unchartered course. Eventually, Andrew declared bankrupt and left the country. Sadly he was the best architect my country has ever produced.

Un-modeled visions

A model is a pattern of a product that does not yet exist. In the case of vision, it is a miniature picture or a representation on a smaller scale of the vision's end product. It represents the ideal or standard that is the target of the vision. Most

> *The fact is many visions end up in un-chartered waters because they failed to chart a proper course for their vision.*

people have a perceptual idea of how their vision will look, and a good visionary will document this part of their vision. However, documenting the vision is not the same thing as modeling a vision. Few visionaries have a model of their vision's end product because this can be an expensive undertaking but vital to the vision's success. *An un-modeled vision is a vision that does not have a practical illustration or representation of its end product.* This could be a technical drawing, an architectural design, an artist picture, a video presentation, a three-dimensional model or a combination of these things. Prospect investors are motivated by what they see, feel and hear; therefore, visions with a model have a greater chance of attracting the resources it requires for its implementation. Also, it essential to the visionary's meditation exercise to realize his or her vision. More on this later.

> *An un-modeled vision is a vision that does not have a practical illustration or representation of its end product.*

A relatively unknown CEO of an organization I am familiar with, I will call Sea breeze (SB), had a two-million-dollar project that this organization planned to accomplish in three years. Before CB started to raise the money for their project, this organization documented the vision, created a project proposal, and built a model of the vision. After three years, CB had the funding and the people to build their project. Their vision was successful because they had all the right ingredients to get it started and moving. People who saw their model display, which was featured in a prominent area of their building, were motivated to support the vision because they could see what they were building. This organization's success was no accident but the product of a well-modeled vision. Consequently, I have also come across many other such projects that are struggling to find support for their vision because they have no model of their vision. People are left trying to imagine what their organization is trying to build, which leaves their vision open to uncertainty and speculation.

Some concluding thoughts

Pitfalls are sure to be part of the process of any vision. While it is possible to avoid these common pitfalls that can plague a vision, never the less some pitfalls are difficult to avoid, especially when you have a disadvantage that is inherent to your vision. Depending on your vision's size and nature, these barriers or stumbling blocks can occur at any time during the implementation or construction of the vision. The key here is not to consider these pitfalls as setbacks but as setups for a comeback. I have known visionaries that have overcome tremendous barriers to see the fulfillment of their vision. I have also learned of visionaries who have been overwhelmed by a pitfall and are still awaiting their vision's realization.

We must realize that no pitfall is ever permanent or lasting unless we make it permanent. A vision will always find another way of being fulfilled despite the situation. Every experienced mother knows that once you are pregnant with a baby, you will experience birth pangs in the course of the nine months while the child is in gestation. No mother abandons her child because of these birth pangs, no matter how painful they become. Pitfalls are like these birth pangs of which are part of the process of the vision being birthed. Few remember these birth pains when the vision is finally birthed.

There is a 5-acre resort project that took over 30 years to realize in my country. An island was created in a lagoon in our City to build a 5-star resort with enough space for other commercial developments. Three previous developers tried to complete the project but failed. Just about all of the factors (pitfalls) listed above were responsible for this vision failure. There was a lack of investment, and the vision was unchartered and unmodelled. Finally, when the new developer came in some 25 years later, they did everything right. They formed a local company with shareholders and launched the project properly with our Government support. The project was professionally planned, phased, funded, and built. Vast advertising billboards of the project were installed outside the site and alongside the main road. It took two years to complete the project, and when it was completed, it was soon a financial success.

The vice of character is the unshakable and unbreakable ground we often call ourselves that will break during the process of vision

CHAPTER EIGHT

The Vices of Vision

A vice can be defined as a common fault in something (a problematic area.) Vision in itself does not have a fault, but it is the visionary or recipient of vision that has the faults because of our imperfect character and because we live in a flawed environment. In television, when we a fault in our transmission at one of our remote mountain sites, inevitably someone will ring up and complain. The picture is transmitted from our master control room is always perfect because we are constantly monitoring it. Therefore, we always know that the fault is at the remote transmission site where that person lives. So we immediately proceed to that site and fix the problem, which is usually a receiving antenna or receiver that has gone down. This is like vision; the vision is always perfect at the source but the receiver at the end, the person who has the fault.

> A vice can be defined as a common fault in something (a problematic area).

These faults are the vices of vision that are readily a source of contention, frustration, and misunderstanding for the visionary and or recipient of the vision. Let us examine some of these vices and consider how we should react.

The vice of timing

Every vision has an appointed time of fulfillment. It is not possible to do it earlier, and it is not possible to do it later. There is always the right time to do it. King Solomon, a Bible man of great wisdom, said, "Everything under the sun has a time of fulfillment." Some visions may not even be for the present time and could well be sometime in the future. *It is a common mistake among visionaries and recipients to rush out and start the vision out of its appointed time.* As a result, the visionary or recipient crashes, and they become discouraged and begin to doubt if the vision was right in the first place. The question is, how do we know the correct timing of a vision? The answer is we do not know; that is why timing is a vice of vision. It is one of those factors we simply cannot control. When the vision is ready to manifest, it will surely let you know, and it will not tarry beyond its appointed time. Indeed, the vision never goes beyond its appointed time; someone will somehow, and somewhere fulfill it.

The vice of glory

Has this ever happened to you? You made or bought something nice like cake and left it in the kitchen or your office, and someone else ate it or took it. We all know the feeling of disappointment and anger

> *The vice of timing is to rush out and start the vision out of its appointed time.*

when this happens, this also occurs with vision. *You come up with the vision, and someone else runs with it and fulfills it and reaps all the profits and rewards.* They take the glory that was due to you. In other situations, you think you were the first to come up with the vision, but you find out later that someone else beat you to it. This is the vice of glory. You can never hold down vision; it has a way of slipping away from you. What is the advice in this case, "let it go!" If it had been meant for you to do it, you would have done it. There will always be other visions. There is a plaque I often see displayed in homes that says, "If you love something let it go, and if it comes back to you, then you were meant to have it."

The vice of burden

I have already dealt with the unpredictable nature of financial costs of a vision, but that is not a vice of vision. *The vice of burden is that personal price that is commonly associated with carrying and implementing the vision.*

> *The vice of glory where you come up with the vision and someone else runs with it, fulfills it, and reaps all the profits and rewards.*

Every vision has a personal cost to the visionary, and that cost will often extend to the family members and friends of the visionary and other recipients. I may be taking this to the extreme, but never the less, it frequently happens. Vision has driven people to alcohol, others to drugs, and others to family and marital breakups. Now I am not referring to evil visions, but I am speaking about good and ordinary visions. The pressure and the commitment that the vision will bring can sometimes be too much for the person to handle. The cause often has to do with our lack of wisdom or understanding or unwillingness to let go. Be sensitive to recognize the points at which you need to ease off and have a break. You will be surprised that this often the last thing on the agenda of a visionary.

The vice of vanity

The vice of burden is that personal price that is commonly associated with carrying and implementing the vision.

Not every vision we will receive is good and beneficial. Sometimes the visions we will receive will have a fine line between sanity and insanity. Some of them will be conspicuously bad or evil. There is no shortage of examples of evil visions driving evil people around the World in our time and even here in our small remote region of the Pacific. This is another of the vices of vision. It has a vanity to it. *The vice of vanity is the evil side of vision that can end up controlling the visionary.* How do you think wars, genocide, mass suicides, apartheid, discrimination, and racism come about? It starts from an evil vision from an evil man who often begins with a false or deceptive idea. An atheist will lack the understanding and power to counteract the spiritual forces behind an evil vision. The damage that the evil forces behind it can inflict will be uncontrollable and immeasurable without a real belief in

GOD/UNIVERSE and His power. Stay clear of evil people and their evil visions and connect yourself to GOD/UNIVERSE, and you shall obtain promising visions.

The vice of wealth

Not every vision is profit-orientated. There are many charitable visions about us. But this is not what I am referring to here.

> *The vice of vanity is the evil side of vision that can end up controlling the visionary.*

The vice of wealth has to do with the precarious nature of vision. Most people embark on a vision because of its lucrative promises. They hope they will become rich and prosperous from it, and there is nothing wrong with this. However, we all know too well how unpredictable life can be, and the same vision we hoped would improve our condition makes it worse or benefits someone else instead. Vision can bring bad fortunes to some people. Now I do not believe in chance and never will, so I tend to put these bad fortunes on our own poor planning and bad decisions. As I have said, environmental factors can complicate things but should never destroy the end result of the vision if we persevere on and complete the vision.

The vice of distortion

Have you ever started with something pure and innocent, and it ended up distorted and out of kilt? *The vice of distortion has to do with the distortions or perversions that people create in vision. When*

> *The vice of distortion has to do with the distortions or perversions that people create in vision. When the vision is first received, it is in its purest state, but as time progresses, people often distort or pervert the vision.*

The vice of distortion has to do with the distortions or perversions that people create in vision. When the vision is first received it is in its purest state, but as time progresses, people often distort or pervert the vision. There are various reasons people do this, and I will not touch on these as I am assuming that you understand human nature. The fact is it happens, and it happens quite frequently in the realm of vision. People distort or pervert visions from their original purpose to twist it to their advantage or someone else's advantage or to wreck it or annihilate it. The courts are continually litigating over such matters, and wars are fought continuously over such things because people by nature are never satisfied with what they have. In such circumstances, you can persist on and breakthrough it, or it may be better to back off or give up the vision for a time.

The vice of character

> *The vice of deformity has to do with the distortions and perversions that people create in vision.*

The general and express purpose of most visions is to change or improve the condition of something. That something must also include the visionary's character or the character of the recipient of the vision. Most visionaries and recipients do not expect to personally change in the process of vision, but the fact is they do. Some changes will be for good, and some changes will be for the bad. However, most visions lead to the improvement of the person's character and life. I have rarely ever met a person who has completed a vision that had not personally testified that they have changed for the better as a result of the vision. *The unshakable and unbreakable ground we often call ourselves will break during the process of vision.* So expect everything to change, including yourself and your family and your friends, and not to mention the recipients of your vision.

The vice of cost

Sometimes despite our best efforts to secure funding to implement the vision, it just does not work out. *The vice of cost refers to these situations where you end up having to fund your own vision.* Sometimes vision demands that we make the ultimate sacrifice. Selling everything I own to get the seed money to start the vision or putting a mortgage on my house to obtain the financing and borrowing off friends and family to start. Many people cannot produce proposals to find sources, or they may not have a financial background, but they have a property that they are prepared to give up or mortgage to some lending institution to start their vision. In other cases, investors hold out until they know what you are ready to sacrifice or give up something. After all, if you are not prepared to give what you have, why should other people share what

> *The vice of character is the unshakable and unbreakable ground we often call ourselves will break during the process of vision.*

they have to help you? This is a fair expectation. You will be surprised at how many people started this way. The bottom line is; if you believe in your vision, then the cost is really immaterial. The benefits and rewards of your vision promises should cover your costs if you have done your homework.

The vice of duplicity

> *The vice of cost refers to these situations where you end up having to fund your own vision.*

It is a property of vision that it tends to duplicate itself despite our best efforts to stop this from happening. Thus, it often happens in duplicate visions that the person who had the vision first has an advantage because they were first in the field, the territory, or the market. *This is the vice of duplicity in that the person holding a duplicate vision stands at a naturally disadvantaged position.* It is a common thing in any country to find people in duplicate visions in the same or similar service or business in the same community, town, or city; this is done to foster competition and promote Entrepreneurship, but there are a few exceptions. The point here is that while your vision may not be unique in the sense that the vision has already been implemented, it does not mean the vision is inferior or that it is not for you, or that it won't be successful. Many people make a success of duplicate visions despite their disadvantaged position. Your vision could well have components in it that are better than your competitors, and the market may just need another duplicate. Don't give up.

Some concluding thoughts

> *The vice of duplicity refers to the disadvantages that are created by duplicate visions.*

I have brushed over many areas that could have been explained in much more detail, but I believe that I will be taking from you the very experiences and victories that GOD/UNIVERSE and the dreamers who inspired you want you to personally have, not that we want to be mean to you. As much as I would like you to avoid all these vices, some vices, unfortunately, are necessary not necessarily for the vision but also for the visionary's perfection. When I look back at some of my own experiences, I can now say with a clear and joyful conscience, "I needed that thank you."

At the end of the vision process, there will be a crown of glory and magnificent rewards, which you rightly deserve, but there are three plausible positions that you will arrive at the end of your vision that I would like to tell you something about. At the end of the process of vision, you can say like King Solomon had said, "all is vanity!" meaning it was meaningless OR second you can say like most people say, "it was worth it all!" yes the pains, the headaches, etc. compared to what I now see and have OR lastly you can say as Yeshua The Master (Jesus Christ) and my hero said, "So likewise you, when you have done all those things which you are commanded, say, 'We are unprofitable servants. We have done what was our duty to do'."

When you think that it's in your reality now, you will attract it to you, but if you think of it as something that will come to you later, it will never come. "Later" doesn't exist.

CHAPTER NINE

The Incubation of Vision

How many of you reading have watched the movie the Secret and perhaps have read the books *the Science of Getting* Rich by Wallace D Wattles or Napoleon Hill *Think and Grow Rich*? Elementary reading for those who want wealth and prosperity. These masterpieces teach six universal laws, which is vital to understand the incubation of a vision;

1. The Law of Energy.
2. The Law of Vibration.
3. The Law of Attraction.
4. The Law of Visualization.
5. The Law of Sowing and Receiving.
6. The Law of Gratitude.

However, there is a seventh law that none of these books teach, which you shall learn here.

7. The Law of Agreement.

I shall explain the laws first and then teach you how to implement them to realize a vision. This section assumes that you have fulfilled the practical orientation of vision outlined in the previous chapters and have studied the wisdom to avoid the pitfalls. The information on each of these laws is standard reading in prosperity and growth courses, and I will borrow the information from these Masters.

The Law of Energy

The Universe consists of 99.9 percent of empty space, and it is not empty. The law of energy (alternatively the law of substance) states; that the Universe is filled with a formless substance of which, in its original state, permeates, penetrates, and fills the interspace of the Universe. This substance is inexhaustible and has no final state. It has been called by many names, dark matter, dark energy, vibrations, sound, the Matrix, Supreme Intelligence, Gia, Ensof, the Tao, and God. I have found the best description of it from the teaching of the Tao Te Ching;

Since before time and space were, the Tao is. It is beyond is and is not...It flows through all things, inside and outside, and returns to the origin of all things. It is like a well: used but never used up. It is like the eternal void: filled with infinite possibilities...	"The Tao there was something formless and perfect before the universe was born. It is serene. Empty. Solitary. Unchanging. Infinite. Eternally present. It is the

mother of the universe. For lack of a better name, I call it the Tao... *Since before time and space were, the Tao is. It is beyond is and is not...It flows through all things, inside and outside, and returns to the origin of all things. It is like a well: used but never used up. It is like the eternal void: filled with infinite possibilities...* The world is formed from the void, like utensils from a block of wood. The universe follows the Tao. The Tao follows only itself... It is hidden but always present. The Tao is infinite, eternal. Why is it eternal? It was never born; thus, it can never die. Why is it infinite? It has no desires for itself; thus, it is present for all beings. The Master stays behind; that is why she is ahead. She is detached from all things; that is why she is one with them. Because she has let go of herself, she is perfectly fulfilled... Tao Te Ching. I don't know who gave birth to it. It is older than God."

There is more on the Tao;

"The Tao doesn't take sides; it gives birth to both good and evil. The Master doesn't take sides; she welcomes both saints and sinners. The Tao is like a bellows: it is empty yet infinitely capable...The Tao is called the Great Mother: empty yet inexhaustible; it gives birth to infinite worlds. It is always present within you. You can use it any way you want.... The more you use it, the more it produces; the more you talk of it, the less you understand. Hold on to the center."

This energy is inexcusable; it cannot be used up or destroyed. It is neither created nor destroyed. It is the stuff from which the entire Universe was created and from which it draws its strength to continue its eternal expansion. It is present everywhere and in every living and non-living thing. We are made from it in the image of Him who created us. It a neutral substance; it has no form, no chemistry, no electrons, no name or title. It just exists and is always present. It is not GOD or the Universe. Thus, it takes no sides; both good and evil proceed from it. Amazingly it can be transformed into anything we desire. Every Great Master who has lived knew about it embraced its knowledge and used it to form their kingdoms. The knowledge of it was hidden from us for millenniums and passed down through secret organizations that later could not keep it hidden anymore. But what exactly is it? It is simple; it is Pure and tranquil Energy unlike anything in the physical world. Therefore, it operates through defined laws, which we shall learn of next.

The Law of Vibration

> Basically, this law says that everything in the Universe moves and vibrates - everything is vibrating at one speed or another. Nothing rests. Everything you see around you is vibrating at one frequency or another, and so are you, and Science confirms this phenomena.

This is an unchangeable fact; our lives are governed by laws whether we like it or not. Laws govern the Universe! When we bring our lives into harmony with the laws, we will enjoy more of life. One of these powerful laws is the law of vibration, which is a direct extension of the law of energy. I quote from the internet; "The Law of Vibration states that anything that exists in our universe, whether seen or unseen, broken down into and analyzed in its purest and most basic form, consists of pure energy or light which resonates and exists as a vibratory frequency or pattern. All matter, thoughts, and feelings have their own vibrational frequency. The thoughts, feelings, and actions we choose also have their own particular rates of vibration." *Basically, this law says that everything in the Universe moves and vibrates - everything is vibrating at one speed or another. Nothing rests. Everything you see around you is vibrating at one frequency or another, and so are you, and Science confirms this phenomena.*

"Science reveals that everything in the manifest universe is ultimately composed of packets of energy; quantized units vibrating at specific frequencies. Quantum physicists have shown that, although matter may appear to be solid when you look at it through a high-powered microscope so that it is broken down into its smallest components: molecules, atoms, neutrons, electrons, and quanta (the smallest particles measurable), it is ultimately mostly empty space interspersed with energy. So, in essence, everything is comprised of energy and empty space. Everything that appears solid is the frequency of the vibration of the energy that makes it up. An interesting fact about this is that the denser the object, the higher the speed of vibration. At the same time, the lower the density of an object is, the lower the speed of vibration." In essence, everything is a vibration or a frequency moving at speeds faster than the speed of light, but what exactly is it in our finite mind? A vibration is basically a sound. When the vibration is gibberish or meaningless, it is a noise that usually manifests as empty space or chaos. Still, when it is intelligent or ordered, it manifests as matter both animate and inanimate we can relate. This is the foundation on which a vision becomes a reality through this next law.

The Law of Attraction

Simply put, the Law of Attraction is the ability to attract into our lives whatever we are focusing on. The Law of Attraction uses the power of the mind to translate whatever is in our thoughts and materialize them into reality. In basic terms, all thoughts turn into things eventually. If you focus on negative doom and gloom, you will remain under that cloud. If you focus on positive thoughts and have goals that you aim to achieve, you will find a way to achieve them with massive action. The rule is negative energies attract negative energies, and positive energies attract positive energies.

This the psychology behind it. I quote from the internet again. "For us, thought is where it all begins. As your conscious mind dwells habitually on thoughts of a certain quality, these become firmly embedded within the subconscious mind. They become the dominant vibration. This dominant vibration sets up a resonance with other similar vibrations and draws them into your life. This is easier to understand if you consider that from the metaphysical view, the whole universe IS MIND. In turn, your vibrations affect everything around you – your environment, the people and animals around you, the inanimate objects, even the seemingly 'empty' space, and they, in turn, affect you. Your feeling at the present moment dictates your vibration. It is said that feeling is a word to define conscious awareness of vibration. So, your feeling at the moment is your vibration you are in, which sets up things of like nature. *Positive feelings = positive circumstances, negative feelings = negative circumstances."* For clarity, think of vibrations as intelligent sounds people, or things can read or relate. These sounds are everywhere around us.

> Positive feelings = positive circumstances,
> negative feelings = negative circumstances.

These vibrations (sound) will set up resonance with whatever possesses identical frequency. In other words, your thoughts are inseparably connected to the rest of the universe. "Like attracts like." As you choose good thoughts, more good thoughts of the same nature will follow, and you will also be in vibrational harmony with others with like thoughts. Our energy needs to vibrate at the same frequency as what it is we are seeking. Likewise, we can "tune" our thoughts, feelings, and actions. We can immerse ourselves in the vision we're seeking. We have to adjust our environment so that our vision can flourish. This brings us to the next law, the Law of Visualization.

The Law of Visualization

The law of visualization states that whatever we picture clearly in our mind and focus our thought power on it will eventually materialize. It is part of the law of vibration that is a proven scientific technique. Here a definition of this technique from Wikipedia. "Visualization is any technique for creating images, diagrams, or animations to communicate a message. Visualization through visual imagery has been an effective way to communicate both abstract and concrete ideas since the dawn of humanity. Examples from history include cave paintings, Egyptian hieroglyphs, Greek geometry, and Leonardo da Vinci's revolutionary methods of technical drawing for engineering and scientific purposes. Visualization today has ever-expanding applications in science, education, engineering (e.g., product visualization), interactive multimedia, medicine, etc. Typical of a visualization application is the field of computer graphics. The invention of computer graphics (and 3D computer graphics) may be the most important development in visualization since the invention of central perspective in the Renaissance period. The development of animation also helped advance visualization."

Visualization is really quite simple. *The basic idea behind visualization is that in order to get what you want in life, you have to be able to picture that thing clearly in your mind and in as much detail as possible.* Visualization techniques have been used by successful people to visualize their desired outcomes for ages. Elite athletes use it today. The super-rich uses it. And peak performers in all fields now use it. We all have this tremendous power, but most of us have never been taught to use it effectively. We will come to its practical application later.

The Law of Sowing and Receiving

This is an ancient law of nature that GOD first introduced to mankind in the Book of Genesis. "While the earth remaineth, *seedtime and harvest*, and cold and heat, and summer and winter, and day and night shall not cease" verse 8:22. Seedtime and harvest is the law of sowing and reaping. Thus when Paul wrote, "Whatsoever a man soweth, that shall he also reap," he simply extended and applied that law of nature to man's moral and physical nature. We all reap what we have sown. If a man wastes his strength in riotous living, in overindulgence in work or play, or is careless about wasting his nerve force and strength, he will reap the wastrel's harvest. Even if he lives to a ripe old age, he will have far less vigor than had he lived a moderate life and conserved his physical resources.

> Your treasure is your vision. Where your treasure is where you will sow your time, resources, and efforts. If there is no sowing in your vision, there will be no reaping.

Life is about sowing and reaping. It is about planting seeds and harvesting. What kind of seeds are you sowing? Your life is like a field or a garden, and every day you are sowing seeds in that field/garden, whether or not you realize it. Your thoughts are seed. Your words are a seed. Whatever becomes of your life, what becomes of you, is first sowed in your mind and in your heart. The good seed produces good fruit, and the bad seed produces bad fruit, the Master Yeshua taught. This law is relatively easy to understand, but how does it apply to vision. I can explain its connection through this explanation of Yeshua, "For where your treasure is, there your heart will be also" Mathew 6:21. Your treasure is your vision. Where your treasure is where you will sow your time, resources, and power. If there is no sowing in your vision, there will be no reaping. It is as simple as that. I will show you how this all works soon.

The Law of Gratitude

Learning and practicing the law of gratitude complement and enhance the law of attraction and the law of sowing and reaping. As this man correctly observed, "Grateful people are as fertile fields; they give the received back tenfold" August von Kotzebue. Gratitude is defined as an attitude of being thankful, being ready to show appreciation for anything received. It also includes returning the kindness. Related terms include thankfulness, thanks, appreciation, and indebtedness. Thus, the law is composed in this way. The Law of Gratitude states that action and reaction are always equal and extend in opposite directions. This is who it works; a grateful attitude is like a powerful force. If we allow ourselves to feel grateful for what we have, we will be rewarded in return. If you express gratitude, you will attract more of the reason for expressing gratitude. It can be life-transforming. Since your mind attracts more of what you focus your mind on, the more gratitude you express, the more you will be able to express. Likewise, the more misery you think about, the more you will attract into your life.

To put it in another way, the easiest way to make your blessings count is to count your blessings, which is how you activate this law. Acknowledging the good things you already have in your life is of the essence because whatever you appreciate

> To put it in another way, the easiest way to make your blessings count is to count your blessings, and that is how you activate this law.

and give thanks for will grow stronger in your life. That is the seed you need to start watering first before visualizing the result. The Universe responds quickly to a heart that is truly thankful. Gratitude leads to greatness. It can literally turn what you have into more than enough, jobs into joy, chaos into order, uncertainty into clarity, and bring peace to an otherwise chaotic day. But if we are not grateful, discontent is pre-programmed, and we will have bad experiences in our life. We automatically direct our attention to deficiencies and lack. With a negative mindset, we will focus on the bad and on lack. If we focus on our life's inadequacy, we program our brain to perceive only the discontent and attract it in our life. A person with a grateful mind, however, is confident of receiving the best. A grateful person looks forward to the future and is ready to accept challenges and take them positively to grow. What this attitude does in vision is create an open door where the flow of resources can come to your vision. Without gratitude, nothing opens, and nothing comes. The final law and the most neglected is the law of agreement.

The Law of Agreement

The Law of Agreement says that as we lend our agreement to any belief, we reinforce it and make it stronger. Alternatively, as we refrain from lending our agreement to an idea that isn't likely to give us the results we're looking for, we dilute it and weaken its power over us and everyone else simultaneously. The Master Yeshua framed the law in this way "Again I say to you, that if two of you agree on earth about anything that they may ask, it shall be done for them by My Father who is in heaven" Mattityahu (Matthew) 18:20. *I am not referring to a legal agreement or contract but the power of agreement between two or more people to move the supernatural world to create the thing you wish to see.* This is what Yeshua is talking about.

> I am not referring to a legal agreement or contract but the power of agreement between two or more people to move the supernatural world to create the thing which you wish to see come to pass.

The truth is nothing will ever happen when there is no agreement in the spiritual dimension. As a law in itself, the Spiritual is always first and higher than the natural. When there is no involvement and agreement in this area, the natural world does not respond. In the situation of an atheist, it just makes it more complicated but not impossible, and somewhere along the journey, someone in the chain of the command will inevitably perform this because it is indispensable when we seek to release the creative power of the uncreated formless substance in the first law (the Law of Substance). The signing of the legal contracts to build the vision results from an agreement in the spirit. When there are no agreements in the spirit, nothing will happen that is determined to occur. Whether you accept this or not, the Father or, if you prefer, the Universe does not respond to visions that loath or disregard the source of all things. Who are we but a vapor in the wind, here today and gone tomorrow? I remind you again we just the vessels in which a higher power wishes to bless or provide for many others. The vision is given for the good and benefit of many. The Source must be involved in the vision if it is to be successful, and through the power of agreement, we can bring the substance to create and build the vision.

The Implantation

What is to come next is a practical lesson that is indispensable to birthing a vision. This is not a theoretical exercise. The steps outlined are sure to achieve the project regardless of your situation, your vision's size, or your vision's cost. Here are the steps to putting the above into action. We will start from the very beginning and work through the laws. You need to go through these phases and tick each step after completion and note that some steps have no expiration date. Phase one to eight encompasses all the chapters you have read in this book. Phase nine and ten implements the implantation stage.

Phase One

Commit to educating yourself. Understand the Law of Energy, Vibration, and Attraction. I have provided a guide; there is so much more on these laws to learn from the gurus of this topic. Please understand you are not embarking on a religious education but on a journey of discovery that will open doors and opportunities for you that you would otherwise never discover in this lifetime. This initial step is not an exercise of chance or probability because these laws are as certain and as precise as the laws that govern the path of the sun, moon, and stars. We don't have to guess if the sun, the moon, and the stars will rise tomorrow; we know without a doubt they will be there. In the same expectation, we must realize internally what has been given for our growth and prosperity. If you are not convinced about this, it is pointless to go to step two.

Phase Two

Identify your passion. What do you want to do or achieve in this life or time? I am not talking about your profession or occupation; we all need a job to put food on our table and feed a family. I am specifically referring to what is on your heart. Your innermost belly. Please take some time out of your busy schedule and answer that question; if you do not, vision will not come, let alone accomplish one. When you have found your heart and prepared it, you are ready to receive a vision from above. Let's assume that you have identified your passion.

Phase Three

Expect to receive and download the vision if you have not already. Specifically, I ask, what comes naturally to your mind? What do you see happening out there? Does something need to be fixed, changed, improved, or invented that you have a passion for? Fix that area on your mind and expect the solution as your vision. Thank GOD/UNIVERSE for trusting you with the vision. Express your gratefulness through your day/week because not all parts of the vision come at once and ask for the wisdom and the strength, and courage to complete the vision. Acknowledge that GOD/UNIVERSE has entrusted you with this mission. The involvement of the divine is paramount at all phases.

Phase Four

Write down the vision – put it on paper or electronic storage and draw up a picture or diagram. This is just a preliminary picture of what you have received on which you can build on later. Visualize with your mind what has been shown to you. Activate the law of visualization. Don't be intimidated or afraid of what you see because if it were not meant to be for you to accomplish it, you would not receive it. You must understand it is your destiny, and it will haunt you for the rest of your life until it is completed. Understand this clearly, no man, army, force, or power can stop a vision whose time has come. And it is never too late! Age is meaningless.

Phase Five

Do your homework – get the facts and information you need. Think of yourself in the place of a potential investor and ask the questions you believe they will want to be answered. The very same questions you would like to be answered. Specifically, try to answer all the why, how, when, and where questions. When you have obtained all the facts, don't be put off by the cost and the enormity of the information to digest and organize. As they say, Rome was not built in a day. Every vision has a provision (investor or financier). Know it will take time and commitment, and sacrifice.

Phase Six

Draw up a project proposal and model or picture of the project. You can do this or have someone else do it for you. The project proposal is a business plan and financial plan containing the explanation, strategy, goals, and project figures. It is indispensable to the formation of your vision. It is usually intended for the investor or the bank, or both. This is the party who eventually will make a legal agreement. If you fund your vision, then do the above for yourself and those who run with the vision. Don't shortcut this crucial stage. It is inviting confusion and failure.

Phase Seven

Come to an agreement with two or three people involved in your project for the desired outcome in the name of the Source after you have a physical copy of the project. Sit the people down who you are involved with and explain the vision to them. Win them over or do what is necessary to gain their approval and support. Activate the law of Agreement in your favor and steed. Have them commit to the project somehow, even if it is to just pray for you or be an encourager.

Phase Eight

Schedule seven days of meditation to activate the law of attraction. The forces of the Universe do not just assist you because you have an excellent project. You must activate it. If you do not, it will delay or slow down your project. Activating the law of attraction brings your project into the stream of the supernatural world. The real and unseen world that forms everything around you. Find a time out of your busy schedule to meditate at a specific time and make sure you won't be interrupted. You need about 1-2 hours per day. Realize everything in the supernatural is done in the present tense – the infinite now. You must understand nothing happens in the future; the future happens now. What you do in the now activates the present. There are ten steps in this phase, and you need to follow the instructions carefully. Quickly read through it first and familiarize yourself.

1. Find a quiet meditation spot. It can be anywhere. This place will be your "meditation spot" for the week. It is not good to use multiple locations; it disturbs the flow. Make sure it is a comfortable and clean place. Take a copy of the project proposal and its pictures with you. Place it in front or next to you.

2. Sit down or lie down; whatever position makes you relaxed. You can use a yoga mat and meditation position if you like. Most people prefer to lie down.

3. Place your hands in a comfortable position and close your eyes. Listen to your breathing and heartbeat for a few minutes. Now proceed to empty your mind of the preoccupations of your day. Imagine a peaceful location you have been to before. Remember the feelings of that place. See yourself there. When negative thoughts appear, reject them straight away. Speak to them like your speaking to a person. Tell them to go away.

4. Create in your mind positive, self-empowering statements that uplift and inspire you; for example, I am happy, I am peaceful, I am successful, I am wealthy, etc. Let the sentence be the short version of what you desire. Repeat these sentences to yourself audibly or silently in your head until you feel positive and uplifted. Take all the time you need. You must be in the right feeling.

5. After being in your place of happiness and positive affirmation for 10-15 minutes, empty your mind of the images of the happy or peaceful location you are at and now imagine empty dark space, for example, the image of orbital space or a dark room. It must be dark and empty, and trust me; nothing is going to jump on you from the dark.

6. This is the image and location of the formless substance inside and outside you in every empty spot. Try not to think about its composition but rather submerse in that empty space (the formless substance or the Tao). Flashes of light may appear across your eyelids; they are normal. That is the energy field of your mind you are experiencing.

7. After being in that spot for 5-10 minutes, open your eyes, pick up the project's images, and look intensely at them. If there is more than one image, study them all with your eyes. Make a clear mental picture of the entire project in your mind. Take your time. Make the image in your head as vivid as possible. See the details. Memorize the moment.

8. After forming the images, close your eyes and return to the dark place and now bring the pictures of the project to bear upon the formless substance. Make a mental picture of what it is you wish to have. See it before your eyes and imagine that you already are in a position of whatever it is you want.

See yourself in the project, walking around, and feel the joy and excitement of the accomplishment. See it as happening now. The feeling is what matters. See the project before your eyes and imagine the thing in which you wish to create or produce completed. Try to see the image in bright colors. See details and feel how good it feels to have what you are expecting. Feel how happy you are and smile. Smiling gives you an even stronger feeling of happiness, and your energy is elevated, and you will be a super-strong magnet to what you are focusing on. *When you think that it's in your reality now, you will attract it to you, but if you think of it as*

> When you think that it's in your reality now, you will attract it to you, but if you think of it as something that will come to you later, it will never come. "Later" doesn't exist.

something that will come to you later, it will never come. "Later" doesn't exist. Only now exists, and your visualizations must always be in the present tense. Research has revealed that images or scenes that are accompanied by intense emotion will stay locked in our memory forever. The more passion, excitement, and energy you muster during visualization, the more powerful the results will be.

9. Express thankfulness for the project. Thank GOD/UNIVERSE for the funding (a grant or a loan), for the right people to fund it, for the right partners and friends, for the quick approvals, for the right staff and workers, for the right location and suppliers, for the right time to start the project, etc. Be specific and even name the amount you need, how many staff and the persons you want, etc. Do this for at least 5-10 minutes. The powers at be like specifics. Speak if you need to or shout it out, it does not matter. After you have done this, remain in the thankfulness attitude for the rest of the day and complete the final stage.

10. Sow a one-time monetary seed for the project and expect nothing back in return. I mean, not even a thank you. Ask GOD/UNIVERSE to lead you to where you should sow your seed and let it be done without no one knowing it was you. Give whatever amount the Universe impresses upon you to plant. Note it is not about the amount that is important; it is an exercise of faith and obedience to draw the favor/blessing/mercy of GOD/UNIVERSE. A seed is required to be sown for there to be a harvest. The rule is simple - No seed, no harvest! If you are serious about your vision, then planting a seed or making the sacrifice is not even a consideration.

That completes the process. Note you do not need to repeat all the steps during the next six days; repeat only the steps required to fuel the vision, for example, steps 2-9. After seven days, if you feel you must continue, then do so. At the end of the process, it is essential you now listen out for the cues/clues on the next direction you must take. The people you need to approach and talk to about the vision and project for funding, advice, guidance, recommendations, support, etc. It can come from any direction and any person. Be open and expecting as they say, "GOD/UNIVERSE works in mysterious ways."

SUMMARY

Dreamers move people, but visionaries move mountains. The driving force behind any successful person in the past or the present or the future has been and is and will be V Power. The most powerful thing that a man can have is a vision. If you want your personal life transformed, get a vision. If you want to transform a community or a society, or a nation, give people a vision. The most dangerous thing you can personally do to yourself is to become a visionary. Perhaps you have noticed I have deliberately not defined what vision is until this point because to define it ahead of the volume you have read would be sheer folly. Therefore what is vision? The Concise Oxford dictionary defines vision as, "act or faculty of seeing; thing or person seen in a dream or trance; foresight or good judgment in planning." Management people see vision as setting goals and objectives. Vision is much more than this and much greater than this. Vision is the POWER and ENERGY of the SOUL. It is what drives and energizes people who move mountains. Vision is not a force in that it is neither good nor evil. Nor is it foresight or good judgment in that it is not intuition. Anyone can receive a vision, but not anybody can become a visionary!

> *Dreamers move people, but visionaries move mountains.*

In the right minds, the power of vision will improve and benefit humanity, and in the wrong minds, it will destroy and degrade humanity. When vision has a GOD/UNIVERSE factor in it, it will create destiny. A visionary will have many visions, but only a few of these visions will ever make it into the hallmarks of history and only those visions that make a humane impact that people will remember in the generations to come. There are no secrets to successfully fulfilling a vision. It is merely acquiring the necessary knowledge of vision and understanding the character, logistics, properties, nature, and process of vision. Vision is a metamorphosis activity. It goes through various changes to arrive at its desired end, and it is not understanding how these changes affect vision and the visionary and its recipients where we face the greatest problems. Finally, let me define another of the remaining factors that I have not defined that could only be defined at the end of the book. A visionary is not a person who receives visions. Many people receive visions. There are also many gurus and spiritualists who fall into this category. *A visionary is a person who OPERATES in the power of vision and CREATES visions that move mountains.* They are the people who create the today we live in tomorrow.

> *A visionary is a person who OPERATES in the power of vision and CREATES visions that move mountains.*

YOU CAN BECOME ONE!

ABOUT THE AUTHOR

NO MANS ZONE was founded on the 70th Jubilee year 2009, the Jewish year 5769.

The Purpose of NMZ is set forth in these Scriptures;

- NMZ Vision: Yeshayahu (Isaiah) 40:1-9; Yechezkel (Ezekiel) 37.
- NMZ Mission: Yeshayahu (Isaiah) 61; Yirmeyahu (Yirmeyahu (Jeremiah) 31.
- NMZ Goal: Mattityahu (Matthew) 10:5-10; Marqus (Mark) 16:15-18.

NMZ RELEASES

NOTES

VPOWER

NOTES

For further information contact

nmz@nomanszone.org

Printed in Great Britain
by Amazon

cdbef230-5e6a-4394-9a21-d1e4fdfc7e28R01